JEWISH VEGETARIAN COOKING

A wealth of recipes which combine heritage and tradition with compassion, and use natural wholefood ingredients to create dishes which will be enjoyed by everyone.

Recipes illustrated on cover:
1. Pesach Chocolate Nut Squares (page 123)
2. Gemüse Kugel (page 52)
3. Russian Berry Kissel (page 93)
4. Spinach and Cheese Strudel (page 60)
5. Tabooli (page 89)
6. Beetroot Soup (page 37)

In the same series
GREEK VEGETARIAN COOKING
INDIAN VEGETARIAN COOKING
ITALIAN VEGETARIAN COOKING
MEXICAN VEGETARIAN COOKING

JEWISH VEGETARIAN COOKING

The Finest Traditional Recipes, Made Exciting and Original by the Use of Healthy, Natural Ingredients

by

Rose Friedman

The official cookbook of the International Jewish Vegetarian Society

THORSONS PUBLISHING GROUP

First published 1984

Illustrated by Ian Jones

British Library Cataloguing in Publication Data

Friedman. Rose
Jewish vegetarian cooking.
1. Vegetarian cookery   2. Cookery, Jewish
I. Title
641.5'676   TX837

ISBN 0-7225-0910-3

*Published by Thorsons Publishers Limited,
Wellingborough, Northamptonshire, NN8 2RQ,
England.*

Printed in Great Britain by Woolnough Bookbinding Limited,
Irthlingborough, Northamptonshire

5   7   9   11   13   12   10   8   6   4

CONTENTS

I should like to express my thanks:

To Philip Pick, Quentin Coleman and Shirley Labelda at the International Jewish Vegetarian Society Headquarters for their cheerfulness and helpfulness at all times.

To the late Joe Green of Johannesburg who was kind enough to lend me archive material together with his own writings.

To Eveline Bernard, Vera Jonason, Sharon Rosen and Miriam Zimmermann for sharing ideas and recipes with us.

To Professor Reuben Musiker, of the University of the Witwatersrand, for his encouragement and assistance.

To my family, Susan in particular, for all their help.

Rose Friedman

Foreword

Tradition in food is nurtured deep in the human psyche; through home influence and childhood days it casts its spell of happiness and security.

It is in the natural order of things, therefore, that a change in food habits is not easily brought about; the fact that the inherited pattern was not necessarily a good one is usually of little relevance. Most people look back to their childhood with longing, and the food their mothers prepared is usually something that remains near and dear to their hearts. Jewish philosophy has taken this factor fully into account and it has been incorporated into the very fabric of the Jewish faith. Partaking of food is a sacred right, each human body is a temple and the table becomes an altar dedicated to a service of thanksgiving.

It is a point of interest that throughout the Bible the reward for observing the Commandments always refers to the fruits of the earth, the produce of the field and the grain harvest. Not in a single instance is there a promise of flesh to eat as a reward for carrying out the mitzvahs. During the dispersion to many lands, tradition hallowed the various aspects of Jewish foods, which had little or no connection with the settled agricultural life of ancient Israel. The invitation by the publishers for the J.V.S. to produce a traditional cookery book within the context of vegetarianism, was therefore welcomed by the Society as fulfilling the Biblical emphasis of non-flesh foods as a reward, whilst satisfying readers' inherent love of their traditional background. Our publishers have thereby added one more star to their record of publications designed for thinking people who look upon health as a blessing, and a return as far as possible to the appreciation of natural things.

These vegetarian alternatives will enable readers to enjoy the delights of their traditional dishes, knowing that the elimination of flesh foods will be conducive to the good health of their families whilst carrying out the strictest requirements of Kashruth.

Their table will not be marred by violence, but adorned with the peaceful and goodly products of the land, thus hastening the days when 'they shall no longer hurt nor destroy'.

B'tayavon!

PHILIP L. PICK
Hon. Life President
The International Jewish Vegetarian Society

Introduction

Jews are truly an international people and their cuisine reflects the countries and regions in which they have dwelt. Bringing with them their own traditions and customs, they have adapted the ingredients and dishes of these countries and created their own specialities. In some cases the origins of dishes have become lost through transplantation from one country to another. However, two distinct trends are still discernible – the Spanish Sephardim and the European Ashkenazim.

In each country where they have settled, Jews have learned to adapt to the regional foods and climate. In Eastern Europe where the winters were bitterly cold and people were not very wealthy, dishes were adapted that were economical, filling and warming, and that stretched resources. Thus, we find dishes like kneidlach and kreplach, perogen, gefilte fish (for which we have vegetarian recipes), and hearty soups like cabbage and beetroot, cabbage and tomato and krupnik (barley and mushroom). These would be Ashkenazi dishes. The Sephardim (Spanish Jews, originally) and the near Eastern and Middle Eastern Jews have dishes made from the plentiful produce of those regions, such as aubergines (eggplants), and pulses.

Chopped liver and chopped herring, for which we have given vegetarian recipes, feature at many Jewish functions all over the world, although they are European in origin. Galuptzi (Russian stuffed cabbage leaves), Klops (German-Jewish cottage pie), Lechso (Hungarian sautéed peppers, onions and tomatoes) are all examples of Ashkenazi dishes. Avocado soup, now popular in Israel, could have originated in South America. Fritada le Espinaca (spinach soufflé), Mejedra (rice and lentil pilaff), Lahne be Sahem (layered casserole) and Borekas (savoury baked turnovers) are examples of Sephardi dishes. The ubiquitous aubergine (eggplant) features in many Israeli dishes and appears in a number of recipes. Today's shrinking world has brought all the various cultures together in countries like Israel and the United States of America. Many dishes which were once regional have become international.

In Jewish teachings, eating is regarded as a hallowed act, to be accompanied by the recitation of appropriate blessings. Not only Sabbath and Festival feasts, but each meal is a reminder of the bountifulness of the earth's produce for which we express our gratitude with blessings and thanksgiving.

In ancient times the Jews were an agricultural people, their lives revolved around the cycle of sowing, reaping and harvesting their crops; praying for the early rains ('yoreh', the heavy rains towards the end of October) and the latter rains ('malkosh', the downpours of March and April), upon which their harvests depended. Closeness to the earth and reliance on its produce brought about an increased awareness of man's dependence upon the Almighty. Just as the Sabbath is the pinnacle of each week, so do the Festivals crown the seasons at which they appear. Jewish life and tradition is bound up with these occasions which are celebrated in happiness and with thanksgiving to the Almighty. Incorporated within these traditions are the *mitzvot* (good deeds) of hospitality and charity. The Passover Haggadah (prayer book) opens with the invitation,

'Let him who is hungry come and eat. Let him who is needy come and celebrate the Passover.'

We move from one Festival to the next through the year, renewing our spiritual awareness, extending hospitality to friends and relatives.

The Sabbath

Each week we have the privilege and joy of experiencing the beneficient Sabbath – truly the Queen, the 'Bride', as she is called in the Sabbath hymn. It is said that it is meritorious to think of the Sabbath all week. How does one do this? Any delicacy or delicious fruit one sees in the shops should be purchased with Sabbath in mind so that the best and choicest is kept for this day. In the Western world, where we have so much, it is fitting to remember times when people were poor yet, somehow, still managed to honour the Sabbath.

It is said that each person receives an 'extra soul' on the Sabbath, so that he is doubly able to perceive enjoyment and satisfaction, and physical and spiritual nourishment from this most special of days. The prayers, the laws, the rituals, the peace and happiness which descends on the whole family are enhanced by the joyful presentation of delicious meals. The world, with all its distractions and demands is effectively shut out.

Sunset on Friday is the time when the Sabbath commences. As no cooking is permitted, all preparations are made in advance and the prepared food is kept warm. The Friday evening meal might consist of mock chopped liver, soup with lokshen or perogen, a main course of mock chicken casserole or klops with tzimmes, roast potatoes, green vegetables and salads. Fruit compote, or farfel apple tart and sabra ice-cream might be served. Special, sweet, red wine is present on the Sabbath table, together with the two Challahs (Sabbath loaves). Saturday's lunch might be hot, in which case, cholent and knaidel would be eaten. If a cold meal is preferred, it might begin with iced borsht, egg and onion, mock chopped liver or mock chopped herring, cold slices of klops, a variety of salads, followed by Russian berry kissel or orange surprise.

The Festivals

Each Festival brings to mind tastes and smells, sounds and sights, the excitement of the preparations, the participation of the children and the anticipation of the arrival of the guests. When we celebrate the Festivals, we are participating in the history of our people.

Passover is the celebration of our redemption from slavery. Its takes place in the Spring, and was also celebrated as an agricultural harvest festival. An omer (measure) of barley was presented at the Temple in Jerusalem on the second day of Passover. Preparations for this Festival are rigorous. All leaven is banished from the house. Bread is replaced by matzo (unleavened bread) and confectionary is baked with matzo meal, ground hazelnuts, almonds or walnuts and potato flour. Ashkenazim (European Jews) and Sephardim (Spanish and Portuguese Jews) have different customs relating to the consumption of pulses. The Passover recipes given at the back of the book do not include pulses, but reflect the variety of dishes that may be prepared with vegetables, fruit, nuts and matzo.

Summertime sees the celebration of *Shavuoth* or the Feast of Weeks (seven weeks after the second day of Passover). It is also known as Chag HaBikkurim. Not only does it commemorate the Revelation of the Law on Mount Sinai, but it is a celebration of the wheat harvest, which is the last of the grains to ripen, and the commencement of the fruit harvest. In ancient times, on Shavuoth, thanksgiving offerings of bread baked with fine, new flour from the wheat harvest, and offerings of the first ripe fruit were brought to the Temple in Jerusalem. Those who lived near Jerusalem brought fresh figs and grapes, while dried figs and raisins were brought from afar off. These days, synagogues and houses are decorated with leaves, flowers and plants. Schoolchildren bring attractive baskets of fruit to school, which are then taken to charitable institutions. Cheesecakes, cheese blintzes, honey and fruit dishes are very popular.

Rosh Hashonah (The New Year) is celebrated at the beginning of Autumn. It is a time for people to consider their actions and behaviour, and to pray for forgiveness of their sins and for a good year. Symbolic of sweetness, honey cake, tzimmes with carrots, honey and apples are eaten during Rosh Hashonah. A newly-ripened fruit, not yet tasted that season, is served on the second night of Rosh Hashonah, for which a special benediction is said.

Yom Kippur (The Day of Atonement) is the culmination of the Days of Awe, the Ten Days of Penitence that begin with Rosh Hashonah. It is a solemn day of fasting, prayer and repentence. At the conclusion of the Fast, hopeful that their prayers have been heard, family and friends gather together to break their Fast, some with a full scale meal, others with a simple and light repast, such as sponge cake and fruit juices. Thoughts are already turning towards the celebration of the next Festival.

Succoth (Tabernacles) follows four days after Yom Kippur. It is the third of the three pilgrim festivals, the other two being Passover and Shavuoth. Not only is it a harvest festival, but it commemorates the the forty years' wandering in the desert before the entry into the Promised Land. Temporary booths are erected in gardens, roofed over with leaves and branches, and decorated within with flowers, fruit and pictures of the Holy Land. All meals are eaten in the *Succah*, as it is called, where starlight and sunlight filter through the branches over-head. Being the end of the fruit harvest, fruit strudels, tarts and fruit salads play a prominent part in the menu. The seventh, eighth and ninth days of Succoth are known respectively as *Hoshana Rabbah, Shemini Atzeret* and *Simchat Torah* (Rejoicing of the Law). This last day is a special favourite with the children who receive presents of nuts and raisins, sweets and chocolates, symbolic of the sweetness of the Law.

Chanukah, or the Festival of Lights, occurs in December. Latkes (fritters fried in oil) are eaten to remind us of the miracle of the pure oil, of which one day's supply lasted for eight days, during the restoration of the Holy Temple.

Purim, which takes place one month before Passover is a time for joyful merry-making and the sending of cakes, fruit, wine etc., to friends and relations. It is a perennial reminder of a great deliverance from evil during the reign of Ahasuerus. Kreplach and hamantaschen are usually eaten on this Festival.

Among the minor festivals, *Tu Bi'Shvat* celebrates 'the beginning of the season of the budding of the trees', and is also known as 'New Year of the Trees'. A variety of sweets fruits, especially Israeli fruits, such as grapes, raisins, almonds, dates and figs are eaten.

Last, but not least, is *Rosh Chodesh* (New Moon), celebrated in Biblical times as a holiday, but no longer today. Something special, perhaps a favourite hors d'oeuvre or dessert is added to the meal in honour of the New Moon.

By presenting delicious and nourishing menus, we hope to be able to provide you with inspiration to satisfy family and friends and increase your joy by the knowledge that vegetarianism and Judaism are in complete harmony.

The Jewish Kitchen
The Orthodox vegetarian family obviously need not have separate sets of dishes, cutlery and utensils for meat and milk. Naturally, however, separate utensils are required for Passover.

There are certain watch-points that Jewish vegetarians must pay careful attention to. Only kosher parev margarines should be used, as many others contain animal fats or derivatives. Kosher or strictly vegetarian cheese and jellies may be used.

Certain berries and salad greens, and in particular, certain types of lettuce should be scrutinized and thoroughly washed before use, as it is forbidden to eat even the tiniest insect. Pulses, grains and flour should be carefully examined for any sign of insect life. Eggs should be checked for blood spots, and discarded if any are found.

Rose Friedman

1. HORS D'OEUVRES

AVOCADO AND EGG

Imperial (Metric)

2 ripe avocadoes
4 hard-boiled eggs
2 teaspoonsful lemon juice
2 teaspoonsful grated onion
Mayonnaise for blending
Sea salt
Freshly ground black pepper

American

2 ripe avocadoes
4 hard-boiled eggs
2 teaspoonsful lemon juice
2 teaspoonsful grated onion
Mayonnaise for blending
Sea salt
Freshly ground black pepper

1. Mash the pulp of the avocadoes.

2. Mash the hard-boiled eggs.

3. Combine all ingredients and mix well to form a soft purée.

4. Serve chilled and decorated with chopped parsley. Delicious on thin slices of wholemeal bread.

HUMMUS

Imperial (Metric)	American
½ lb (225g) chick peas	1 cupful garbanzo beans
2 fl oz (60ml) olive oil	¼ cupful olive oil
2 cloves garlic, crushed	2 cloves garlic, crushed
Juice of 1 lemon	Juice of 1 lemon
Sea salt	Sea salt
Paprika or cayenne pepper	Paprika or cayenne pepper

1. Soak the chick peas (garbanzos) in water overnight and then rinse well. Cook for about 2 hours until soft. Mash well or put through a blender.

2. Combine with olive oil, garlic, lemon juice and salt, and mix well to form a smooth paste. If dry, add a little more oil.

3. Sprinkle with the pepper and serve chilled, decorated with olives and parsley. Can be served as a dip with crackers.

MOCK CHOPPED HERRING

Imperial (Metric)	American
1 medium aubergine	1 medium eggplant
2 thick slices soft wholemeal bread or challah	2 thick slices soft wholewheat bread or challah
4·6 tablespoonsful cider vinegar for soaking bread	4·6 tablespoonsful cider vinegar for soaking bread
4 hard-boiled eggs	4 hard-boiled eggs
1 medium onion, grated	1 medium onion, grated
2 large apples, grated	2 large apples, grated
1 tablespoonful light Demerara sugar, or less, to taste	1 tablespoonful light Demerara sugar, or less, to taste
1 tablespoonful olive oil	1 tablespoonful olive oil
Sea salt	Sea salt
Pinch ginger	Pinch ginger
Freshly ground black pepper	Freshly ground black pepper

1. Slice the aubergine (eggplant) through lengthwise, oil the cut side and place cut side down in a very hot pre-heated oven 475°F/240°C (Gas Mark 9) for about 20 minutes until the skin has shrivelled.

2. Remove the skin when cool and mash the pulp.

3. Soak bread in vinegar and a little water until soft and mash well.

4. Mash 3 of the hard-boiled eggs finely, reserving the remaining one for decoration.

5. Mince or combine all ingredients into a smooth, moist spread. Add a little more bread to the mixture if necessary.

6. Mash the yolk and white of the remaining hard-boiled egg separately and decorate the spread, garnishing with parsley pieces, slices of cucumber and slices of tomato.

7. Often served on festive occasions spread on *Kichlach*.

MOCK GEFILTE FISH I

Imperial (Metric)	American
½ lb (225g) butter beans soaked	1⅓ cupsful Lima beans, soaked overnight, rinsed and boiled in plenty of water until soft
1 whole carrot,	
2 medium onions, finely chopped	1 whole carrot
½ green pepper, finely chopped	2 medium onions, finely chopped
3 tablespoonsful sunflower oil	½ green pepper, finely chopped
1 small carrot, grated	3 tablespoonsful sunflower oil
1 thick slice soft bread (challah), soaked in water	1 small carrot, grated
3 tablespoonsful oats	1 thick slice soft bread (challah) soaked in water
1½ teaspoonsful sea salt	3 tablespoonsful oats
1 teaspoonful raw cane sugar	1½ teaspoonsful sea salt
½ teaspoonful paprika	1 teaspoonful raw cane sugar
Garlic salt	½ teaspoonful paprika
1 egg	Garlic salt
2 tablespoonsful water	1 egg
Juice of ½ lemon	2 tablespoonsful water
2 heaped teaspoonsful wholemeal flour	Juice of ½ lemon
	2 heaped teaspoonsful wholewheat flour

1. Boil the soaked butter beans with the whole carrot, until soft.

2. Sauté the onions and green pepper in the oil until soft and golden. Add the grated carrot and fry for another 5 minutes.

3. Reserve the liquid from the boiled beans. Mash the beans smoothly. Reserve the whole carrot for decoration.

4. To the mashed beans, add the bread which has been soaked and mashed. Add the sautéed onions, green pepper and carrot, plus the oil in which they were sautéed, and the oats, seasoning and egg.

5. Add the water and 1 tablespoonful lemon juice. Mix everything very well together. The mixture should be fairly firm.

6. Pour some of the reserved bean liquid into a large roasting tin.

7. Form the bean mixture into flat rissole shapes and place in the bean liquid in the roasting tin. (Leave a tablespoonful of bean mix for thickening the sauce.) Bake at 350°F/180°C (Gas Mark 4) for about 30 minutes.

8. Make a sauce by mixing the flour with a little bean liquid and the rest of the lemon juice. Add to the rest of the bean liquid, stirring over a low heat till it thickens. Add the reserved bean mixture to further thicken the sauce.

9. Pour bean sauce over cooked rissoles. Serve with horseradish sauce (chraine).

MOCK GEFILTE FISH II

Imperial (Metric)	American
1 medium aubergine	1 medium eggplant
Sea salt	Sea salt
1 large onion, finely grated	1 large onion, finely grated
1 small carrot, cooked and mashed	1 small carrot, cooked and mashed
1 tablespoonful ground almonds	1 tablespoonful ground almonds
1 oz (30g) soya flour	¼ cupful soy flour
2 oz (60g) wholemeal breadcrumbs for mixture (soft)	1 cupful wholewheat breadcrumbs for mixture (soft)
1 tablespoonful chopped parsley	1 tablespoonful chopped parsley
Freshly ground black pepper	Freshly ground black pepper
1 oz (30g) wholemeal breadcrumbs for coating	½ cupful wholewheat breadcrumbs for coating
Polyunsaturated margarine	Polyunsaturated margarine
Lemon juice	Lemon juice
1 large carrot, cooked	1 large carrot, cooked

1. Peel the aubergine (eggplant) and slice thickly.

2. Sprinkle with salt and leave for about 30 minutes. Rinse.

3. Boil for about 15 minutes.

4. Press the boiled slices between two plates, removing excess liquid.

5. Mash well and mix in the onion, carrot, almonds, soya flour, breadcrumbs, parsley and seasoning.

6. Place in an oiled casserole dish, sprinkle with remaining breadcrumbs. Dot with small pieces of polyunsaturated margarine and add a little water and lemon juice.

7. Bake at 325°F/170°C (Gas Mark 3) for 30 minutes.

8. Decorate with sliced, cooked carrot and serve hot or cold. Traditionally accompanied by horseradish sauce (chraine).

MOCK FRIED FISH

Imperial (Metric)
1 medium aubergine, peeled
Sea salt
3oz (85g) wholemeal flour *or*
    matzo meal
Freshly ground black pepper and
    paprika
1 teaspoonful dried, mixed herbs
2 eggs, beaten
4 fl oz (120ml) sunflower oil

American
1 medium eggplant, peeled
Sea salt
¾ cupful wholewheat flour *or*
    matzo meal
Freshly ground black pepper and
    paprika
1 teaspoonful dried, mixed herbs
2 eggs, beaten
½ cupful sunflower oil

1. Slice the aubergine (eggplant) thinly. Salt on both sides of each slice and leave for 30 minutes.

2. Wash salt off and dry the slices with kitchen paper.

3. Combine the flour or matzo meal with seasonings and herbs.

4. Dip the aubergine (eggplant) first into flour/matzo meal, then into beaten egg and fry in hot oil until golden brown on both sides.

5. Drain on kitchen paper or brown paper.

MOCK CHOPPED LIVER I
(Green Beans and Eggs)

Imperial (Metric)	American
1 finely chopped onion	1 finely chopped onion
1 celery stick, finely chopped	1 celery stalk, finely chopped
1 oz (30g) polyunsaturated margarine	2 tablespoonsful polyunsaturated margarine
2 hard-boiled eggs	2 hard-boiled eggs
6 oz (170g) finely diced, cooked green beans	1 cup finely diced, cooked green beans
Sea salt, freshly ground black pepper, oregano	Sea salt, freshly ground black pepper, oregano

1. Brown the chopped onion and celery in margarine.

2. Mash the hard-boiled eggs.

3. Mix together the onion, mashed eggs, celery, green beans and seasonings. Blend well.

4. Serve cold, decorated with sliced, pickled cucumber, olives or parsley.

MOCK CHOPPED LIVER II
(Aubergine/Eggplant and Eggs)

Imperial (Metric)	American
1 large aubergine	1 large eggplant
3 hard-boiled eggs	3 hard-boiled eggs
3 medium onions, finely chopped	3 medium onions, finely chopped
1 clove garlic, crushed	1 clove garlic, crushed
Corn oil, for frying	Corn oil, for frying
Sea salt and freshly ground black pepper	Sea salt and freshly ground black pepper
½ teaspoonful dried mixed herbs	½ teaspoonful dried mixed herbs
½ teaspoonful dried oregano	½ teaspoonful dried oregano

1. Prick the aubergine (eggplant) with a fork all over and place on a baking tray in a hot oven 425°F/220°C (Gas Mark 7), until skin begins to shrivel (about 20 minutes).

2. Cool, peel and mash.

3. Peel and chop the eggs.

4. Fry chopped onions and garlic in a little oil, to which salt, pepper and herbs have been added.

5. Add mashed, cooked aubergine (eggplant) and brown all together.

6. Drain off excess oil.

7. Blend together all ingredients to form a soft pâté.

MOCK CHOPPED LIVER III
(Kasha, Peas, Nuts and Eggs)

Imperial (Metric)	American
2 large onions, chopped	2 large onions, chopped
2 cloves garlic, crushed	2 cloves garlic, crushed
2 celery sticks, chopped	2 celery stalks, chopped
Vegetable oil	Vegetable oil
1 teaspoonful oregano	1 teaspoonful oregano
Sea salt	Sea salt
Freshly ground black pepper	Freshly ground black pepper
3oz (85g) cooked green peas	½ cupful cooked green peas
3oz (85g) cooked green beans	½ cupful cooked green beans
2 hard-boiled eggs	2 hard-boiled eggs
6oz (170g) cooked kasha (buckwheat groats)	1 cupful cooked kasha (buckwheat groats)
4oz (115g) chopped mixed nuts	¾ cupful chopped mixed nuts
4 fl oz (120ml) hot vegetable stock, or less as required	½ cupful hot vegetable stock, or less as required

1. Sauté the onions, garlic and celery in a little oil, to which the seasonings have been added.

2. Mash the cooked peas, beans and hard-boiled eggs.

3. Combine the kasha and chopped nuts with the mashed mixture and add sautéed onions, garlic and celery. Blend or mouli.

4. Add sufficient hot vegetable stock to mixture to form a moist, smooth pâté.

5. Serve cold, decorated with parsley.

EIER MIT TZIBBALE
(Egg and Onion)

Imperial (Metric)	American
6 hard-boiled eggs, finely mashed	6 hard-boiled eggs, finely mashed
1 small grated onion	1 small grated onion
1 spring onion, chopped	1 scallion, chopped
1 tablespoonful parsley, chopped	1 tablespoonful parsley, chopped
Sea salt, freshly ground black pepper, garlic salt	Sea salt, freshly ground black pepper, garlic salt
Mayonnaise	Mayonnaise
1 teaspoonful tomato purée	1 teaspoonful tomato paste

1. Mix the first four ingredients together very well.

2. Add seasonings and sufficient mayonnaise to combine into a smooth pâté-like mixture. Mix in tomato purée.

3. Decorate with slices of tomato, cucumber, radish and parsley. Serve with crackers.

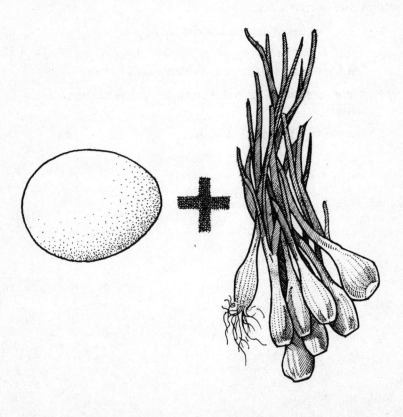

MOCK PETZAH
(Savoury Jelly)

Imperial (Metric)	American
About ¾ lb (340g) of an assortment of cooked, mixed vegetables: peas, green beans, potato pieces and carrot pieces, mushrooms marinated for 30 minutes in lemon juice and mayonnaise, asparagus tips etc.	About 2 cups of an assortment of cooked, mixed vegetables: peas, green beans, potato pieces, carrot pieces, mushrooms marinated for 30 minutes in lemon juice and mayonnaise, asparagus tips etc.
Sliced pickled cucumbers	Sliced pickled cucumbers
Fresh carrot strips	Fresh carrot strips
Tomato slices	Tomato slices
Olives	Olives
3-4 hard-boiled eggs (optional)	3-4 hard-boiled eggs (optional)
2½ pints (1.5 litres) water	6¼ cupsful water
Juice of 2 large lemons	Juice of 2 large lemons
1 vegetable stock cube	1 vegetable stock cube
1 crushed garlic clove	1 crushed garlic clove
1 cupful chopped parsley	1¼ cupsful chopped parsley
1 teaspoonful caraway seeds	1 teaspoonful caraway seeds
1 teaspoonful mixed dried herbs	1 teaspoonful mixed dried herbs
3½ teaspoonsful Agar agar	3½ teaspoonsful Agar agar

1. Arrange the vegetables as attractively as possible in a wetted jelly mould or glass dish. Egg slices may be arranged on the bottom and sides of the mould with slices of pickled cucumber, olives, carrot strips in between, and the cooked vegetables and mushrooms put on the top.

2. Prepare a jelly as follows: boil 2 pints/1 litre (5 cupsful) water with the lemon juice, the vegetable stock cube, crushed garlic, chopped parsley, caraway seeds and herbs for about 30 minutes.

3. Boil the rest of the water in a separate pan and add the agar agar, stirring very quickly. Remove from heat.

4. Add the agar agar mixture to the bigger pan of water. Do not boil again, but simmer gently for 3 minutes.

5. Pour over the prepared vegetables in the mould.

6. Leave to cool, then refrigerate. Turn out and decorate before serving with mayonnaise stars, or avocado pulp beaten with lemon juice, or asparagus spears, olives etc.

TSAVAY
(Yogurt or Sour Cream with Vegetables)

Imperial (Metric)	American
⅔ pint (340ml) plain yogurt *or* sour cream	1 ½ cupsful plain yogurt *or* sour cream
2 cupsful chopped mixed vegetables including tomatoes, cucumbers, celery, grated carrots, spring onions, fresh shredded spinach, cooked or fresh beetroot, radishes, green pepper	2 ½ cupsful chopped mixed vegetables including tomatoes, cucumbers, celery, grated carrots, scallions, fresh shredded spinach, cooked or fresh beet, radishes, green pepper
Sea salt	Sea salt
Freshly ground black pepper	Freshly ground black pepper

1. Combine all the ingredients in a glass bowl and decorate with carrot strips, radish and cucumber slices, tomato wedges and parsley.

2. Serve on lettuce leaves.

2. SOUPS AND
SOUP ACCOMPANIMENTS

CLEAR VEGETABLE SOUP

Imperial (Metric)	American
2 carrots, grated	2 carrots, grated
2 onions, sliced	2 onions, sliced
2 tomatoes, sliced	2 tomatoes, sliced
2 sticks celery, chopped	2 stalks celery, chopped
Chopped parsley, including stems, about 1 cupful	Chopped parsley, including stems, about 1 cupful
1 potato, chopped	1 potato, chopped
1 clove garlic, chopped	1 clove garlic, chopped
Sea salt and freshly ground black pepper	Sea salt and freshly ground black pepper
Herbs	Herbs
10 cupsful water	12½ cupsful water
2 vegetable stock cubes (optional)	2 vegetable stock cubes (optional)
1 teaspoonful Marmite	1 teaspoonful yeast extract

1. Simmer all ingredients in a covered pot for about 2 hours.

2. Strain and adjust seasoning.

3. Serve hot with Kreplach, Perogen, Mandalach, Kneidlach or Lokshen (see page 40).

GEMÜSE SOUP
(Vegetable Soup)

Imperial (Metric)	American
2 carrots, grated	2 carrots, grated
1 potato, grated	1 potato, grated
2 onions, grated or chopped	2 onions, grated or chopped
2 celery sticks, chopped	2 celery stalks, chopped
Vegetable oil	Vegetable oil
2 courgettes, chopped	2 zucchini, chopped
1 ripe tomato, skinned and chopped	1 ripe tomato, skinned and chopped
5oz (140g) brown rice	½ cupful brown rice
1 teaspoonful mixed dried herbs	1 teaspoonful mixed dried herbs
2 vegetable stock cubes	2 vegetable stock cubes
Sea salt and freshly ground black pepper	Sea salt and freshly ground black pepper

1. Lightly fry the carrots, potato, onions and celery in oil for about 5 minutes.

2. Add about 6 pints (2.6 litres/15 cupsful) of water and bring to boil.

3. Add the courgettes (zucchini) and tomatoes and rice and herbs.

4. Simmer for about 1½ hours.

5. Add crushed vegetable stock cubes and simmer for about another ½ hour.

6. Season to taste with sea salt and black pepper.

Note: Leftover soup may be frozen and, when thawed, varied with the addition of fresh peas, cooked kasha, cooked butter (Lima) beans or barley or lentils or whatever you wish.

HOBERNERGROTEN SOUP
(Oats and Vegetable Soup)

Imperial (Metric)	American
2 medium carrots, grated	2 medium carrots, grated
1 large onion, chopped	1 large onion, chopped
1 stick celery, chopped	1 stalk celery, chopped
1 parsnip, grated	1 parsnip, grated
1 potato, grated	1 potato, grated
2 tablespoonsful vegetable oil	2 tablespoonsful vegetable oil
2 vegetable stock cubes	2 vegetable stock cubes
8 cupsful water	10 cupsful water
4oz (115g) *hoobergrits* (oats)	½ cupful *hoobergrits* (oats)
Sea salt and freshly ground black pepper	Sea salt and freshly ground black pepper
1 teaspoonful dried mixed herbs	1 teaspoonful dried mixed herbs

1. Fry the vegetables in oil until soft but not brown.

2. Add the crushed vegetable stock cubes and the water and bring to the boil.

3. Rinse the *hoobergrits* well under running water through a strainer and add to the soup mixture. Add seasoning and herbs.

4. Simmer for about 2 hours.

5. Adjust seasoning and serve hot.

BEAN AND BARLEY SOUP

Imperial (Metric)	American
2 carrots, grated	2 carrots, grated
1 onion, chopped	1 onion, chopped
1 potato, chopped	1 potato, chopped
1 tomato, peeled and chopped	1 tomato, peeled and chopped
1 fl oz (30ml) oil	2 tablespoonsful oil
8 cupsful water	10 cupsful water
1 cupful butter beans (soaked overnight)	1¼ cupsful Lima beans (soaked overnight)
5oz (140g) barley, well rinsed	½ cup barley, well rinsed
Sea salt and freshly ground black pepper	Sea salt and freshly ground black pepper

1. Gently sauté the vegetables (except the tomato) in a little oil until soft.

2. Add the water, the butter (Lima) beans, the well-rinsed barley and the chopped tomato and the seasonings.

3. Bring to the boil and then simmer for about 2 hours in a covered saucepan, stirring from time to time.

SPLIT PEA AND BARLEY SOUP

Imperial (Metric)	American
2 carrots, grated	2 carrots, grated
1 onion, chopped	1 onion, chopped
1 stick celery, chopped	1 stalk celery, chopped
1 fl oz (30ml) vegetable oil	2 tablespoonsful vegetable oil
6 cupsful water	7½ cupsful water
1 tablespoonful chopped parsley	1 tablespoonful chopped parsley
2 vegetable stock cubes (optional)	2 vegetable stock cubes (optional)
1 cupful split peas (soaked overnight)	1 cupful split peas (soaked overnight)
½ cupful barley, well rinsed	½ cupful barley, well rinsed
Sea salt and freshly ground black pepper	Sea salt and freshly ground black pepper

1. Fry carrots, onion and celery in a little oil until soft.

2. Add the water, the chopped parsley, vegetable stock cubes, split peas and barley and bring to the boil. Simmer for about 2 hours until the peas are soft. Season to taste. Add a little water if too thick. Serve hot.

KARTOFFEL SOUP
(Potato Soup)

Imperial (Metric)

1 onion, chopped
1 oz (30g) polyunsaturated margarine
1 carrot, grated
1 stick celery, chopped
3 potatoes, peeled and chopped
3 cups of water
3 cupsful of milk
2 tablespoonsful chopped parsley
Sea salt and freshly ground black
  pepper

American

1 onion, chopped
2½ tablespoonsful polyunsaturated
  margarine
1 carrot, grated
1 stalk celery, chopped
3 potatoes, peeled and chopped
3¾ cupsful of water
3¾ cupsful of milk
2 tablespoonsful chopped parsley
Sea salt and freshly ground black
  pepper

1. Brown the onions in the margarine.

2. Add the carrot, celery and potatoes and bring to the boil with the water and milk. Add the seasonings. Simmer for about 30 minutes.

3. Add the chopped parsley and simmer for a further 10 minutes. Serve garnished with sour cream or plain yogurt if desired.

KRUPNIK
(Barley and Mushroom Soup)

Imperial (Metric)	American
1 oz (30g) polyunsaturated margarine	2½ tablespoonsful polyunsaturated margarine
2 carrots, finely grated	2 carrots, finely grated
1 medium onion, finely chopped	1 medium onion, finely chopped
2oz (55g) chopped mushrooms	¾ cupful chopped mushrooms
7 cupsful water	8¾ cupful water
2 vegetable stock cubes	2 vegetable stock cubes
1 cupful (285g) barley	1¼ cupful barley
Sea salt and freshly ground black pepper	Sea salt and freshly ground black pepper
1 tablespoonful chopped parsley	1 tablespoonful chopped parsley

1. Melt the margarine in a saucepan and gently fry carrots, onion and mushrooms until soft, for about 15 minutes.

2. Add the water and the stock cubes and bring to the boil.

3. Add the barley and the seasonings and simmer for about 1½-2 hours, stirring from time to time. Add some water if too thick.

4. Serve hot, sprinkled with chopped parsley if desired.

MARAK AVOCADO
(Avocado Summer Soup)

Imperial (Metric)	American
2 medium-sized ripe avocados	2 medium-sized ripe avocados
Juice of ½ lemon	Juice of ½ lemon
4 cups vegetable stock	5 cupsful vegetable stock
Sea salt and freshly ground black pepper	Sea salt and freshly ground black pepper

1. Liquidize the avocado pulp (mash it or put it through a sieve if you do not have a liquidizer).

2. Combine all the ingredients and blend well together.

3. Chill well and serve cold. This soup may also be served hot, in which case it is heated up, but not boiled, and a little dry white wine may be added. Serve garnished with a slice of lemon floating on the surface.

CABBAGE BORSHT

Imperial (Metric)	American
1 large beetroot, peeled and chopped	1 large beet, peeled and chopped
1 large onion, chopped	1 large onion, chopped
2 carrots, grated	2 carrots, grated
¼ small, white cabbage, thinly sliced	¼ small, white cabbage, thinly sliced
1 oz (30g) polyunsaturated margarine	2½ tablespoonsful polyunsaturated
7 cupsful water	margarine
2 tomatoes, skinned and chopped	8¾ cupsful water
Sea salt and freshly ground black	2 tomatoes, skinned and chopped
pepper	Sea salt and freshly ground black
2 potatoes, peeled and diced	pepper
Sour cream or yogurt	2 potatoes, peeled and diced
	Sour cream or yogurt

1. Place the beetroot (beet), onion, carrot and cabbage into a saucepan and add the margarine.

2. Cover with water and bring to the boil.

3. Add the tomatoes and seasonings and simmer for about 1½ hours.

4. Add the diced potato and simmer for another ½ hour.

5. Serve hot with sour cream or plain yogurt.

SWEET AND SOUR CABBAGE AND APPLE SOUP

Imperial (Metric)	American
⅓ pint (200ml) tomato juice	¾ cupful tomato juice
2 vegetable stock cubes	2 vegetable stock cubes
6 cupful water	7½ cupful water
1 small white cabbage, shredded	1 small white cabbage, shredded
2 large cooking apples, chopped	2 large cooking apples, chopped
1 medium onion, grated	1 medium onion, grated
Sea salt and freshly ground black pepper	Sea salt and freshly ground black pepper
Honey to taste	Honey to taste
Juice of 1 lemon	Juice of 1 lemon

1. Boil together the tomato juice, vegetable stock cubes and water.

2. Add the cabbage, apples and onion to the boiling mixture and simmer for 45 minutes – 1 hour.

3. Serve hot after seasoning with salt and pepper and adding the lemon juice and a few teaspoonsful of honey, according to taste, to achieve a sweet-sour taste.

CABBAGE AND TOMATO SOUP

Imperial (Metric)	American
1 medium onion, chopped	1 medium onion, chopped
1 fl oz (30ml) sunflower seed oil	2 tablespoonsful sunflower seed oil
3 or 4 medium, ripe tomatoes, skinned and chopped	3 or 4 medium, ripe tomatoes, skinned and chopped
1 small white cabbage, shredded	1 small white cabbage, shredded
Water	Water
1 vegetable stock cube	1 vegetable stock cube
Sea salt and freshly ground black pepper	Sea salt and freshly ground black pepper
Honey to taste	Honey to taste

1. Gently sauté the onion in the oil.

2. Add the tomatoes, cabbage and sufficient water to cover the vegetables.

3. Add the vegetable stock cube and the seasoning.

4. Simmer for about 2 hours.

5. Add a few teaspoonsful of honey if a slightly sweet-sour taste is desired.

BEETROOT SOUP
(Iced or Hot)

Imperial (Metric)	American
4-6 large beetroot	4-6 large beet
8-10 cupsful water	10-12½ cupsful water
Sea salt and freshly ground black pepper	Sea salt and freshly ground black pepper
Juice of 1 lemon	Juice of 1 lemon
Honey to taste (optional)	Honey to taste (optional)

1. Wash and scrub beetroot (beet) very thoroughly.

2. Cook in saucepan with the water, for about 1½ to 2 hours, until soft. Strain off the liquid.

3. Grate the beetroot (beet) when cool and return to liquid (or, if a clear soup is preferred, reserve them for a salad).

4. Season to taste with the sea salt, black pepper, lemon juice and honey. Refrigerate until needed.

5. May be served as it is, garnished with chopped cucumbers and a spoonful of cream. May be served mixed with milk in equal quantities and topped with a spoonful of sour cream or plain yogurt. Sometimes served with a hot boiled potato in the soup.

SCHAV
(Summer Sorrel Soup, Served Cold)

Imperial (Metric)	American
1 lb (455g) sorrel	1 lb schav (sour leaves)
6-8 cupsful water	7½-10 cupsful water
Juice of 1 lemon	Juice of 1 lemon
Sea salt and freshly ground black pepper	Sea salt and freshly ground black pepper
2 eggs	2 eggs
Cream to garnish, or yogurt	Cream to garnish, or yogurt

1. Wash the leaves very thoroughly, cut up roughly and boil in the water for about 20 minutes.

2. Press through a strainer or a vegetable mill.

3. Add the juice of a lemon and season with salt and pepper and put back to boil.

4. Beat the eggs well.

5. Remove boiling liquid from heat, allow to cool slightly, then stir beaten eggs in gradually.

6. Cool and refrigerate. Serve cold, with a spoonful of cream or plain yogurt.

PEACH OR PLUM SUMMER SOUP

Imperial (Metric)	American
8 ripe peaches or 12 ripe sweet plums	8 ripe peaches or 12 ripe sweet plums
4 cupsful water	5 cupsful water
Demerara sugar, to taste	Demerara sugar, to taste
Sea salt	Sea salt
Cream or plain yogurt	Cream or plain yogurt

1. Boil the peaches or plums in the water until they are soft.

2. Remove stones and force pulp through a sieve or vegetable mill.

3. Return pulp to liquid.

4. Add sugar and salt to taste.

5. Refrigerate and serve chilled with cream or plain yogurt.

COLD FRUIT SOUP ·

Imperial (Metric)	American
3lb (1.4 kilos) assorted fruits (berries, cherries, apricots, pears, plums, peaches)	3 pounds assorted fruits (berries, cherries, apricots, pears, plums, peaches)
4 cupsful water	5 cupsful water
2 tablespoonsful lemon juice	2 tablespoonsful lemon juice
Cinnamon	Cinnamon
Honey	Honey
Sweet red wine (optional)	Sweet red wine (optional)
1½ teaspoonful arrowroot	1½ teaspoonful arrowroot
Sour cream or plain yogurt	Sour cream or plain yogurt

1. Slice the larger fruit and pit but do not peel.

2. To the water, add lemon juice, cinnamon, and 1 or 2 teaspoonsful of honey, as well as the wine if desired.

3. Simmer all the fruit in this liquid until soft.

4. Purée the fruit through a sieve or a vegetable mill.

5. Combine the arrowroot with a little cold water, add to the puréed fruit mixture and bring to the boil, stirring all the while. Add some water if too thick.

6. Simmer for a short while. Refrigerate. Serve cold with cream or plain yogurt.

Soup Accompaniments:

LOKSHEN AND FARFEL

Imperial (Metric)	American
½ teaspoonful sea salt	½ teaspoonful sea salt
½ lb (225g) 81 per cent wholemeal flour	2 cupsful 81 per cent wholewheat flour
3 eggs	3 eggs
8 fl oz (225ml) cold water	1 cupful cold water

1. Stir about ½ teaspoonful of sea salt into flour. Make a well in centre of flour.

2. Beat the eggs slightly and pour into the well of flour. Add the water.

3. Mix to a stiff dough, adding a little more flour if necessary.

4. Roll out paper thin on a floured surface, then fold up into a roll and cut into strips, either very fine strips for soups, or slightly wider strips for lokshen puddings.

5. Allow strips to dry before storing in an airtight container.

6. For *Farfel* do not roll out the dough, but break into small balls. Allow them to dry and then grate on a fine grater. When quite dry, store in an airtight container.

7. These Lokshen or Farfel are dropped into soup, traditionally clear soups, and boiled for about 15 minutes in the soup before serving.

MANDALACH
(Soup Nuts)

Imperial (Metric)	American
½ teaspoonful sea salt	½ teaspoonful sea salt
About 6oz (170g) 81 per cent wholemeal flour	About 1½ cupsful 81 per cent wholewheat flour
2 eggs	2 eggs
1 tablespoonful corn oil	1 tablespoonful corn oil

1. Stir sea salt into the flour. Make a well and add the slightly beaten eggs and oil.

2. Make a soft, firm dough. Add a little more flour if sticky.

3. Knead well and roll out into long ropes. Cut into tiny pieces about the size of half an almond.

4. Spread on well-greased baking pan and brown in oven until golden, at 375°F/190°C (Gas Mark 5).

5. To be served with clear soups or green pea soup. Use as croûtons.

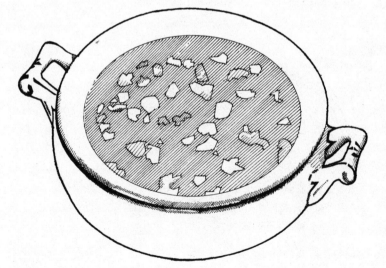

KNEIDLACH
(Soup Dumplings)

Imperial (Metric)	American
2 eggs	2 eggs
4 fl oz (100ml) water	½ cupful water
2 tablespoonsful corn oil	2 tablespoonsful corn oil
Sea salt and freshly ground black pepper	Sea salt and freshly ground black pepper
2 teaspoonsful cinnamon powder	2 teaspoonsful cinnamon powder
Matzo meal	Matzo meal

1. Beat the eggs very well until light and frothy.

2. Add the water and the oil and beat well again.

3. Add the seasoning and gradually add matzo meal to form a soft consistency, like oatmeal porridge.

4. Place in the refrigerator for about 1 hour.

5. Have a large pot of boiling, salted water on the stove and form the kneidlach mixture into small balls. Drop the balls into boiling water. Boil for about 20 minutes. Allow plenty of room for expansion as they almost double in size. Traditionally served in clear soup on Friday nights and Festivals.

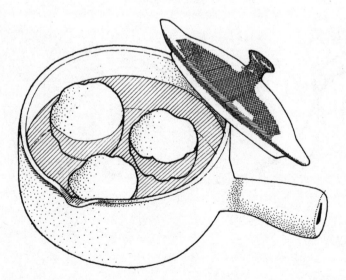

PEROGEN
(Savoury Filled Pasties)

Imperial (Metric)	American
½lb (225g) 81 per cent wholemeal flour	2 cupsful 81 per cent wholewheat flour
2 teaspoonsful baking powder	2 teaspoonsful baking powder
Sea salt and freshly ground black pepper	Sea salt and freshly ground black pepper
Onion salt	Onion salt
Garlic salt	Garlic salt
1 egg	1 egg
2 fl oz (60ml) corn oil	¼ cupful corn oil
Water to mix to a soft dough	Water to mix to a soft dough
½ quantity filling mixture (see note)	½ quantity filling mixture (see note)

1. Mix together the flour, baking powder, and a pinch of the seasonings and make a well in the centre.

2. Pour into the well the lightly beaten egg and the corn oil and mix in with a spoon to form a dough. Add a little water if too dry.

3. Knead the dough and then divide into small pieces which are then rolled out very thinly. When rolled out each piece should measure approximately 5 x 5 inches (13 x 13 cm).

4. Place a heaped tablespoonful of desired filling in the centre of the square, moisten fingers with water and pinch the edges of the dough closed over the filling.

5. Brush with beaten egg. Bake at 375°F/190°C (Gas Mark 5) until golden brown.

6. Serve in Clear Vegetable Soup (page 29) or hot Beetroot (Beet) Soup (page 37).

Note: For filling, use Lentil Koklaten (page 49) or Nut Klops (page 47) recipes from the Main Course Section, adding a little water or vegetable stock to moisten the filling. A mashed hard-boiled egg may also be added to the filling.

KREPLACH
(Small Savoury-filled Dough Pockets)

Imperial (Metric)	American
Sea salt	Sea salt
½ lb (225g) 81 per cent wholemeal flour	2 cupsful 81 per cent wholewheat flour
3 eggs	3 eggs
1 tablespoonful water	1 tablespoonful water
½ quantity filling mixture (see note)	½ quantity filling mixture (see note)

1. Mix the salt into the flour. Make a well in centre of the flour. Beat the eggs slightly and pour into the well of flour.

2. Add the water. Knead the ingredients into a stiff dough.

3. Roll out thinly onto floured surface. Cut into small squares.

4. Place a heaped teaspoonful of your chosen filling into centre of each square.

5. Moisten fingertips and seal into small triangles.

6. Drop into boiling salted water and remove with a slotted spoon after about 15 minutes.

7. Serve hot in clear soup.

Note: For the filling, use Lentil Koklaten or Nut Klops from Main Course Section, adding a little water or vegetable stock to moisten the filling.

3. Main Courses

CASHEW NUT CASSEROLE

Imperial (Metric)	American
3oz (85g) polyunsaturated margarine	1/3 cupful polyunsaturated margarine
1½oz (45g) 81 per cent wholemeal flour	6 tablespoonsful 81 per cent wholewheat flour
1 teaspoonful sea salt	1 teaspoonful sea salt
Freshly ground black pepper	Freshly ground black pepper
⅔ pint (340ml) vegetable stock	1½ cupsful vegetable stock
8 fl oz (230ml) milk	1 cupful milk
3oz (85g) chopped mushrooms	1 cupful chopped mushrooms
1 tablespoonful chopped onion	1 tablespoonful chopped onion
Vegetable oil	Vegetable oil
5oz (140g) cashew nuts	1 cupful cashew nuts
2oz (55g) stoned, sliced black olives	½ cupful pitted, sliced black olives
White wine (optional)	White wine (optional)

1. Melt the margarine in a saucepan and blend in the flour and salt and pepper.

2. Remove from the heat and slowly blend in the vegetable stock and the milk.

3. Bring to the boil, stirring all the time.

4. Sauté the onions and mushrooms in a little oil and add to the sauce.

5. Add the cashew nuts and the sliced olives. (At this point a little wine may be added if desired.)

6. Simmer gently for about 20 minutes, stirring occasionally.

7. Serve hot with brown rice and a green salad.

KLOPS I

Imperial (Metric)

½ lb (225g) continental (brown) lentils, soaked overnight and rinsed well
1 pint (570ml) water *or* vegetable stock
2 medium onions, sliced
2 cloves of garlic
1 medium carrot, grated
1 fl oz (30ml) corn oil
3oz (85g) chopped mushrooms
1 teaspoonful yeast extract
1 tablespoonful tomato purée
1 tablespoonful chopped parsley
2 tablespoonsful wheatgerm
Sea salt and freshly ground black pepper
Chilli powder *or* cayenne pepper
2 fl oz (60ml) vegetable stock
1 tablespoonful lemon juice
1oz (30g) grated cheese
3oz (85g) fresh wholemeal breadcrumbs

American

1 cupful brown lentils, soaked overnight and rinsed well
2½ cupsful water *or* vegetable stock
2 medium onions, sliced
2 cloves of garlic
1 medium carrot, grated
2 tablespoonsful corn oil
1 cupful chopped mushrooms
1 teaspoonful yeast extract
1 tablespoonful tomato paste
1 tablespoonful chopped parsley
2 tablespoonsful wheatgerm
Sea salt and freshly ground black pepper
Chilli powder *or* cayenne pepper
¼ cupful vegetable stock
1 tablespoonful lemon juice
¼ cupful grated cheese
1 cupful fresh wholewheat breadcrumbs

1. Bring the soaked lentils to the boil in the water or vegetable stock and simmer until tender, about 30 minutes.

2. Sauté the onions, crushed garlic cloves and grated carrots in the oil until soft, about 15 minutes.

3. Add the chopped mushrooms and cook for a further 10 minutes.

4. Mash the cooked lentils with potato masher or purée through vegetable mill.

5. Combine all ingredients together, except for the grated cheese and breadcrumbs. Place mixture into a well-greased casserole and sprinkle with lemon juice.

6. Bake at 375°F/190°C (Gas Mark 5) for about 45 minutes. Sprinkle with grated cheese and breadcrumbs about 20 minutes before the end of cooking time.

KLOPS II

Imperial (Metric)	American
4 oz (115g) mixed nuts, finely chopped (cashews, hazelnuts, walnuts)	1 cupful mixed nuts, finely chopped (cashews, hazelnuts, English walnuts)
1 large onion, finely grated	1 large onion, finely grated
1 oz (30g) soya flour	¼ cupful soy flour
1½ oz (45g) *All Bran*	⅓ cupful *All Bran*
½ oz (15g) fresh wholemeal breadcrumbs	¼ cupful fresh wholewheat breadcrumbs
2 eggs	2 eggs
1 tablespoonful chopped parsley	1 tablespoonful chopped parsley
Sea salt and freshly ground black pepper	Sea salt and freshly ground black pepper
1 teaspoonful yeast extract	1 teaspoonful yeast extract
1 pint (570ml) tomato juice	2½ cupsful tomato juice

1. Combine all ingredients, except the tomato juice, and mix well.

2. Place in a greased casserole dish and pour over the tomato juice.

3. Bake at 350°F/180°C (Gas Mark 4) for 45 minutes. Cover casserole halfway through if it seems to be drying out.

4. Serve with brown rice, vegetables and salads. May also be served cold, in slices, with salads and mayonnaise.

Note: For decoration, line the bottom and sides of the casserole with onion rings, courgette (zucchini) rings and celery strips, before placing the mixture into the casserole.

A topping for the Klops mixture may be made by sautéing finely chopped or minced mushrooms with 1 onion and spreading it over the mixture before baking in the oven.

KLOPS III

Imperial (Metric)

4oz (115g) Tvp mince (hydrated according to directions on packet)
1 medium onion, finely chopped
1 clove garlic, crushed
3 or 4 medium, ripe tomatoes
1 carrot, grated
2 tablespoonsful chopped parsley
1oz (30g) fresh wholemeal breadcrumbs *or* 2oz (55g) cooked, brown rice
1 teaspoonful yeast extract
2 teaspoonsful dried mixed herbs
1 teaspoonful paprika
1 egg (optional)
2 tablespoonsful sunflower oil
3 or 4 parboiled potatoes for topping
Vegetable stock

American

1 cupful Tvp mince (soy protein) (hydrated according to directions on packet)
1 medium onion, finely chopped
1 clove garlic, crushed
3 or 4 medium, ripe tomatoes
1 carrot, grated
2 tablespoonsful chopped parsley
½ cupful fresh wholewheat breadcrumbs *or* ⅓ cupful cooked, brown rice
1 teaspoonful yeast extract
2 teaspoonsful dried, mixed herbs
1 teaspoonful paprika
1 egg (optional)
2 tablespoonsful sunflower oil
3 or 4 parboiled potatoes for topping
Vegetable stock

1. Sauté the finely chopped onion and crushed garlic in the oil until soft.

2. Peel and chop the tomatoes and add to onion and garlic.

3. Combine all ingredients except potatoes in a bowl and add a little vegetable stock to moisten and soften.

4. Place in well-greased casserole dish and pour over a little hot vegetable stock (about ½ pint/285ml/1⅓ cupsful).

5. Slice the potatoes thinly and place in rings to cover the mixture completely. Dot with margarine, and sprinkle with sea salt and ground black pepper.

6. Bake at 350°F/180°C (Gas Mark 4) for about 45 minutes or until potatoes are crispy brown on top.

Note: Toppings may be varied. Mash the potatoes, instead of slicing them and combine with a little milk, salt and pepper and spread over the klops.

Steamed puréed cauliflower, blended with a little milk and flour and seasoned with nutmeg and topped with grated cheese is delicious spread on top of the klops.

KOKLATEN I
(Lentil Rissoles)

Imperial (Metric)	American
½ lb (225g) continental (brown) lentils, soaked overnight, rinsed well	1 cupful brown lentils, soaked overnight, rinsed well
1 pint (570ml) water or vegetable stock	2½ cupsful water or vegetable stock
2 medium onions, chopped	2 medium onions, chopped
1 fl oz (30ml) corn oil	2 tablespoonsful corn oil
2 cloves of garlic	2 cloves of garlic
3oz (85g) chopped mushrooms	1 cupful chopped mushrooms
1 teaspoonful yeast extract	1 teaspoonful yeast extract
1 tablespoonful chopped parsley	1 tablespoonful chopped parsley
Sea salt and freshly ground black pepper	Sea salt and freshly ground black pepper
Chilli powder or cayenne pepper	Chilli powder or cayenne pepper
3oz (85g) fresh wholemeal breadcrumbs	1 cupful fresh wholewheat breadcrumbs
2 tablespoonsful wheatgerm	2 tablespoonsful wheatgerm
1 egg	1 egg
Polyunsaturated margarine	Polyunsaturated margarine
Lemon juice	Lemon juice

1. Bring the soaked lentils to the boil in the water or vegetable stock and simmer until tender, for about 30 minutes.

2. Sauté the onions in a little oil and add crushed or sliced garlic and fry gently for another 10 minutes.

3. Add the chopped mushrooms and cook for a further 10 minutes. Remove from the heat.

4. Mash the cooked lentils with a potato masher or purée through a vegetable mill.

5. Combine the lentils, mushroom and onion mixture, yeast extract, parsley, seasoning, breadcrumbs, wheatgerm and egg.

6. Shape the mixture into rissoles, and place on a greased baking tin. Dot each rissole with a little margarine and a squeeze of lemon.

7. Bake at 375°F/190°C (Gas Mark 5) for 30 minutes. (Do not allow to become dry.)

8. Serve with home-made tomato or mushroom sauce and vegetables of your choice.

KOKLATEN II
(Vegetable Rissoles)

Imperial (Metric)	American
2 medium onions, finely chopped	2 medium onions, finely chopped
1 large stick celery, finely chopped	1 large stalk celery, finely chopped
2 medium carrots, finely grated	2 medium carrots, finely grated
6 oz (170g) green peas, cooked	1 cupful green peas, cooked
6 oz (170g) French beans, cooked	1 cupful snap beans, cooked
2 eggs, beaten	2 eggs, beaten
1 teaspoonful mixed herbs	1 teaspoonful mixed herbs
1 teaspoonful yeast extract	1 teaspoonful yeast extract
1 tablespoonful tomato purée	1 tablespoonful tomato paste
1½ oz (45g) *All Bran*, crushed	½ cupful *All Bran*, crushed
Sea salt and freshly ground black pepper	Sea salt and freshly ground black pepper
1 fl oz (30ml) corn oil	2 tablespoonsful corn oil
Seasoned flour (optional)	Seasoned flour (optional)

1. Gently fry until soft the finely chopped onions, celery and carrots.

2. Mash with a potato masher or purée through a vegetable mill the cooked peas and beans.

3. Combine all the ingredients except the seasoned flour and mix very well.

4. Place in the refrigerator for about 30 minutes

5. Form into rissoles, which may be dipped into seasoned flour.

6. Place on greased baking tray and dot each rissole with a little polyunsaturated margarine or a few drops of oil.

7. Bake at 350°F/180°C (Gas Mark 4) for 30-40 minutes.

8. Delicious served with home-made tomato or mushroom sauce, baked potatoes and salads.

KASHA KOKLATEN
(Roasted Buckwheat Rissoles)

For the kasha:

Imperial (Metric)	American
1 onion, finely chopped	1 onion, finely chopped
2oz (55g) chopped mushrooms	½ cupful chopped mushrooms
2 tablespoonsful sunflower oil	2 tablespoonsful sunflower oil
6oz (170g) buckwheat groats	1 cupful buckwheat groats (kasha)
1 egg, beaten	1 egg, beaten
¾ pint (426ml) hot vegetable stock	2 cupsful hot vegetable stock
1 teaspoonful yeast extract	1 teaspoonful yeast extract
Sea salt and freshly ground black pepper	Sea salt and freshly ground black pepper

1. Lightly fry the onion and mushrooms in the oil in a saucepan, until soft.

2. Add the buckwheat groats and beaten egg. Stir for a few minutes.

3. Pour the vegetable stock over the kasha mixture, add the yeast extract and the seasoning.

4. Simmer with lid on for about 20 minutes until all the liquid has been absorbed.

For the koklaten:

Imperial (Metric)	American
1oz (30g) finely chopped, mixed nuts	¼ cupful finely chopped, mixed nuts
1 egg, beaten	1 egg, beaten
1 teaspoonful mixed herbs	1 teaspoonful mixed herbs

1. Combine the kasha mixture with the nuts, the beaten egg and the herbs. Mix well and shape into rissoles.

2. Bake on greased baking tray for 20-30 minutes at 350°F/180°C (Gas Mark 4), until crisp and brown. Serve with vegetables and salads.

GEMÜSE KUGEL
(Rainbow Vegetable Kugel)

Imperial (Metric)	American
3 medium carrots, grated	3 medium carrots, grated
1 small cauliflower	1 small cauliflower
3 medium potatoes	3 medium potatoes
6 oz (170g) fresh green peas	1 cupful fresh green peas
1 grated onion	1 grated onion
1 large courgette, grated	1 large zucchini, grated
2 sticks celery, finely chopped	2 stalks celery, finely chopped
1 ripe tomato, skinned and chopped	1 ripe tomato, skinned and chopped
2 oz (55g) polyunsaturated margarine	¼ cupful polyunsaturated margarine
Sea salt and freshly ground black pepper	Sea salt and freshly ground black pepper
2 tablespoonsful sour milk	2 tablespoonsful sour milk
2 eggs, beaten	2 eggs, beaten
1 tablespoonful curd cheese	1 tablespoonful curd cheese
2 oz (55g) grated Gouda cheese	½ cupful grated Gouda cheese
1 oz (30g) grated nuts *or* sesame seeds (optional)	2 tablespoonsful grated nuts *or* sesame seeds (optional)

1. Steam the carrots, cauliflower, potatoes and green peas until tender.

2. Meanwhile, sauté the grated onion, courgette (zucchini), chopped celery and chopped tomato in the margarine. Season with salt and pepper.

3. Grease an ovenproof dish. Mash the steamed carrots and add the sour milk, salt and pepper and a little beaten egg to form a soft consistency. Press into the bottom of the dish.

4. Mash the steamed cauliflower and add the curd cheese plus 1 tablespoonful of grated Gouda cheese, salt and pepper and a little more of the beaten egg. Press on top of the carrot mixture in the dish.

5. Mash the peas, add a little more beaten egg and seasoning and press on top of the cauliflower.

6. Mash the potatoes, add more grated cheese and egg and press on top of the peas.

7. Cover with the onion, courgette (zucchini), celery, tomato mixture. Add the remainder of the grated cheese and grated nuts or sesame seeds if wished.

8. Bake at 350°F/180°C (Gas Mark 4) for ½ hour until golden-brown.

9. May be decorated with carrot strip lattices dipped in egg with sliced steamed brussels sprouts in each little square.

GEDEMPTE GEMÜSE MIT NISSLACH
(Vegetable and Nut Loaf)

Imperial (Metric)	American
1½oz (45g) polyunsaturated margarine	3 tablespoonsful polyunsaturated margarine
2 large carrots, finely grated	2 large carrots, finely grated
2 sticks celery, finely chopped	2 stalks celery, finely chopped
2 medium onions, finely chopped	2 medium onions, finely chopped
2oz (55g) chopped mushrooms	¾ cupful chopped mushrooms
5oz (140g) ground mixed nuts	1 cupful ground mixed nuts
1 tablespoonful chopped parsley	1 tablespoonful chopped parsley
4oz (115g) fresh wholemeal breadcrumbs	1 cupful fresh wholewheat breadcrumbs
2 eggs, beaten	2 eggs, beaten
2 teaspoonful yeast extract	2 teaspoonsful yeast extract
Sea salt and freshly ground black pepper	Sea salt and freshly ground black pepper
1 teaspoonful thyme	1 teaspoonful thyme
⅓ pint (200ml) vegetable stock	¾ cupful vegetable stock

1. Melt the margarine and lightly fry the grated carrots, celery, onions and mushrooms.

2. Add the ground nuts and the parsley and sauté for another 5 or 10 minutes.

3. Remove from heat and add the rest of the ingredients. Mix well.

4. Bake in well-greased loaf tin at 350°F/180°C (Gas Mark 4) for about 45 minutes.

5. Serve hot with tomato or mushroom sauce and vegetables or salad.

GEMÜSE TORTE MIT KAESE
(Vegetable and Cheese Pie)

For the pastry:

Imperial (Metric)	American
2oz (55g) polyunsaturated margarine	¼ cupful polyunsaturated margarine
4oz (115g) wholemeal flour	1 cupful wholewheat flour
1 egg yolk *or* 4 teaspoonsful water	1 egg yolk *or* 4 teaspoonsful water
Sea salt	Sea salt

1. Rub the margarine into the flour until the mixture resembles fine breadcrumbs.

2. Add the egg yolk or water and knead slightly until the dough is fairly stiff. Add a little water if required.

3. Roll out and place in a greased pie dish.

For the filling:

Imperial (Metric)	American
1 aubergine	1 eggplant
Sea salt and freshly ground black pepper	Sea salt and freshly ground black pepper
2 onions, chopped	2 onions, chopped
3 courgettes, cut up finely	3 zucchini, cut up finely
3 large tomatoes, skinned and chopped	3 large tomatoes, skinned and chopped
1 small green pepper, diced	1 small green pepper, diced
1 clove garlic, crushed	1 clove garlic, crushed
2oz (55g) grated Gouda cheese	½ cupful grated Gouda cheese
1 11½oz (325g) tin sweetcorn	1 can sweetcorn (2 cupsful)
2 tablespoonsful corn oil (or slightly more if required)	2 tablespoonsful corn oil (or slightly more if required)

1. Peel, slice and salt the aubergine (eggplant) and leave for 30 minutes.

2. Meanwhile, sauté the onions, courgettes (zucchini), tomatoes, green pepper and garlic.

3. Wash the salt off the aubergine (eggplant) and add to the onion mixture and sauté until soft; season to taste.

4. Sprinkle the pie crust with a third of the grated cheese and add half the vegetable mixture, including half the sweetcorn. Sprinkle again with another third of the grated cheese.

5. Add the rest of the vegetable mixture including the remainder of the sweetcorn, and sprinkle the rest of the cheese on top.

6. Bake at 350°F/180°C (Gas Mark 4) for 45 minutes.

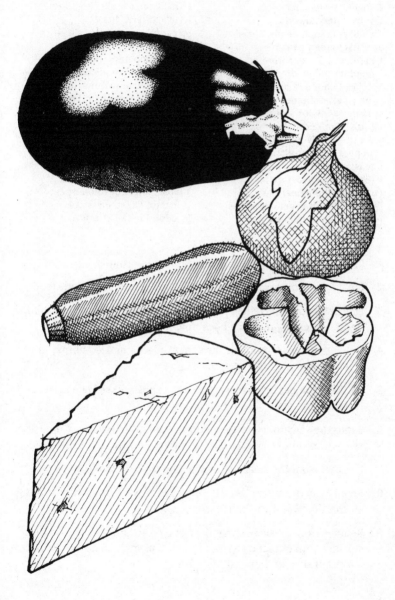

GEMÜSE FLUDEN
(Vegetable Pie in Creamy Sauce)

Imperial (Metric)	American
1 quantity pastry (page 54)	1 quantity pastry (page 54)
4oz (115g) broccoli	1 cupful broccoli
2 small carrots, diced	2 small carrots, diced
1 stick celery, diced	1 stalk celery, diced
3oz (85g) French beans, sliced	½ cupful snap beans, sliced
3oz (85g) green peas	½ cupful green peas
1 medium potato, parboiled	1 medium potato, parboiled
1 medium onion, diced	1 medium onion, diced
1oz (30g) chopped mushrooms	½ cupful chopped mushrooms
½oz (15g) wholemeal breadcrumbs	¼ cupful wholewheat breadcrumbs
Sesame seeds for sprinkling	Sesame seeds for sprinkling
1 fl oz (30ml) corn oil	2 tablespoonsful corn oil
Sea salt, freshly ground black pepper and paprika	Sea salt, freshly ground black pepper and paprika
1 teaspoonful mixed herbs	1 teaspoonful mixed herbs
1 teaspoonful yeast extract	1 teaspoonful yeast extract
1oz (30g) wholemeal flour	3 tablespoonsful wholewheat flour
⅓ pint (200ml) vegetable stock	¾ cupful vegetable stock
⅓ pint (200ml) milk (or water)	¾ cupful milk (or water)
1 egg yolk	1 egg yolk

1. Prepare the pastry and line a greased casserole.

2. Steam the broccoli, carrots, celery, beans and peas until tender.

3. Dice the potato into small pieces and sauté half the chopped onion, the mushrooms and diced potatoes for about 10 minutes.

4. Cut the steamed broccoli into small pieces and combine all the steamed and sautéd vegetables.

5. Sprinkle the pastry base with breadcrumbs and sesame seeds and place all the vegetables in the casserole.

6. Sauté the remainder of the chopped onion in a little oil, and add sea salt, ground black pepper, paprika, herbs and yeast extract.

7. Remove from the heat and stir in the flour to make a roux.

8. Replace on the stove, and add the vegetable stock and milk, stirring all the time until the sauce thickens.

9. Remove from the heat, stir in the egg yolk, return to the heat briefly, stirring. Pour over the vegetables in the pie dish. Bake for about 30 to 40 minutes at 350°F/180°C (Gas Mark 4).

ASPARAGUS PIE

For the dough:

Imperial (Metric)	American
4oz (115g) 85 per cent wholemeal flour	1 cupful 85 per cent wholewheat flour
1 teaspoonful light Demerara sugar	1 teaspoonful light Demerara sugar
Sea salt	Sea salt
2oz (55g) polyunsaturated margarine	¼ cupful polyunsaturated margarine
2 fl oz (60ml) milk, or less	¼ cupful milk, or less

For the filling:

Imperial (Metric)	American
1oz (30g) polyunsaturated margarine	2½ tablespoonsful polyunsaturated margarine
2 medium onions, finely chopped	2 medium onions, finely chopped
2 small tins asparagus pieces	2 small cans asparagus pieces
1 egg	1 egg
2 fl oz (60ml) cream	¼ cupful cream
Freshly ground black pepper	Freshly ground black pepper
2oz (55g) grated Gouda cheese	½ cupful grated Gouda cheese
Paprika	Paprika

1. To make the dough, mix all the dry ingredients together, then rub margarine into the flour until it looks like fine breadcrumbs.

2. Add sufficient milk to form a firm dough. Press the dough into a greased ovenproof dish.

3. For the filling, melt the margarine and sauté the onions until they are transparent and soft. Layer the sautéd onions on the pastry.

4. Drain the asparagus and spread over the onions.

5. Beat the egg until light and frothy.

6. Beat the cream until thick.

7. Fold beaten egg into cream, season with pepper and pour over the asparagus. Sprinkle with grated cheese and paprika.

8. Bake at 425°F/220°C (Gas Mark 7) for approximately 20 minutes until golden-brown.

9. Delicious served with spinach and salads.

BLINIS

For the batter:

Imperial (Metric)	American
2 eggs	2 eggs
6oz (170g) 85 per cent wholemeal flour	1½ cupsful 85 per cent wholewheat flour
Sea salt and freshly ground black pepper	Sea salt and freshly ground black pepper
⅔ pint (340ml) water	1½ cupsful water

1. Beat the eggs until frothy.

2. Add the flour, salt, pepper and a little water gradually, beating well.

3. Add the rest of the water gradually, beating well. The batter should be smooth.

4. Grease a pan lightly with margarine or vegetable oil.

5. Pour in about a tablespoonful of batter and swirl pan to distribute batter evenly. Cook till edges lift up easily. Stack the blinis on a cloth.

For the filling:

Sautéed, chopped onions and mushrooms, *or* mashed, tinned asparagus pieces, *or* cooked, drained seasoned spinach mixed with curd cheese.

Roll up the blinis around some filling and fold like envelopes.

For the sauce:

Imperial (Metric)	American
1oz (30g) polyunsaturated margarine	2½ tablespoonsful polyunsaturated margarine
½oz (15g) 85 per cent wholemeal flour	2 tablespoonsful 85 per cent wholewheat flour
⅓ pint (200ml) milk	¾ cupful milk
Liquid from tinned asparagus *or* from sautéed mushrooms	Liquid from canned asparagus *or* from sautéed mushrooms
2oz (55g) grated cheese	½ cupful grated cheese
Freshly ground black pepper	Freshly ground black pepper

1. Melt margarine and stir in flour to make a roux.

2. Blend in the milk and liquid and stir over heat until the sauce thickens.

3. After the filled blinis have been arranged in a greased casserole, pour the sauce over them and sprinkle with grated cheese and ground black pepper.

4. Bake in oven at 350°F/180°C (Gas Mark 4) for about 15 minutes.

AUBERGINE SOUFFLÉ

Imperial (Metric)	American
2 medium aubergines	2 medium eggplants
1 oz (30g) polyunsaturated margarine	2½ tablespoonsful polyunsaturated margarine
½ oz (15g) 85 per cent wholemeal flour	2 tablespoonsful 85 per cent wholewheat flour
Sea salt and freshly ground black pepper	Sea salt and freshly ground black pepper
½ pint (285ml) milk	1⅓ cupsful milk
4 eggs	4 eggs
6 oz (170g) grated cheese	1½ cupsful grated cheese
1 oz (30g) soft wholemeal breadcrumbs	½ cupful soft wholewheat breadcrumbs

1. Slice the aubergines (eggplants) in half lengthwise and place cut side down on an oiled baking sheet. Bake in a very hot oven, 450°F/230°C (Gas Mark 8) for about 20 minutes, until skin shrivels. Remove the skin and mash the pulp.

2. While the aubergines (eggplants) are baking, melt the margarine in a saucepan.

3. Stir in the flour, salt and pepper to make a roux. Stir in the milk gradually, stirring all the time, until the mixture thickens.

4. Separate the egg yolks and whites and beat up the whites stiffly.

5. Combine the mashed vegetable pulp, the white sauce, cheese and egg yolks. Fold in the stiffly beaten egg whites.

6. Grease a soufflé dish and sprinkle with the breadcrumbs.

7. Pour the mixture into the dish and sprinkle with a little grated cheese if wished.

8. Bake at 375°F/190°C (Gas Mark 5) for about 35-45 minutes, till golden. Serve immediately with a crisp salad.

SPINACH AND CHEESE STRUDEL

For the pastry:

Imperial (Metric)	American
6oz (170g) wholemeal flour	1½ cupsful wholewheat flour
2 tablespoonsful grated Gouda cheese	2 tablespoonsful grated Gouda cheese
½ teaspoonful mixed herbs	½ teaspoonful mixed herbs
4oz (115g) polyunsaturated margarine	½ cupful polyunsaturated margarine
¼ pint (140ml) cold water	⅔ cupful cold water
1 teaspoonful lemon juice	1 teaspoonful lemon juice

1. Mix together the flour, grated cheese and herbs and cut the margarine in and then rub in.

2. Add the water and lemon juice and combine everything to form a soft dough.

3. Roll the dough into a rectangular shape and fold it over twice, press the edges down, turn to the left. Do this twice more and then put the dough into the refrigerator until required.

For the filling:

Imperial (Metric)	American
2 onions, finely chopped	2 onions, finely chopped
1 clove garlic, crushed	1 clove garlic, crushed
1oz (30g) polyunsaturated margarine	2½ tablespoonsful polyunsaturated margarine
2 tomatoes, finely chopped	2 tomatoes, finely chopped
2 tablespoonsful chopped parsley	2 tablespoonsful chopped parsley
Sea salt and freshly ground black pepper	Sea salt and freshly ground black pepper
1 teaspoonful paprika	1 teaspoonful paprika
1 egg, beaten	1 egg, beaten
½lb (225g) curd cheese	1 cupful curd cheese
2oz (55g) grated Gouda cheese	½ cupful grated Gouda cheese
1 tablespoonful tomato purée	1 tablespoonful tomato paste
1lb (450g) cooked spinach, chopped and drained	2 cupsful cooked spinach, chopped and drained

1. Sauté the onions and the garlic in the margarine until golden and add the tomatoes and parsley and seasoning, and gently fry for a few more minutes. Remove from heat.

2. Reserve a little of the beaten egg for brushing the pastry.

3. Mix together the cheeses, the beaten egg, the tomato purée and the spinach and combine with the sautéd onion and tomato mixture.

4. Remove pastry from refrigerator and divide into 4 pieces. Roll each piece out into a rectangular shape.

5. Divide the filling into four and spread evenly, leaving a good margin around the edges. Roll up to form a long roll.

6. Brush with the beaten egg and a little water and oil mixed. Bake on greased baking tray at 400°F/200°C (Gas Mark 6) for about 30 minutes, until golden-brown.

LECHSÓ

Imperial (Metric)	American
1 onion, chopped	1 onion, chopped
1 fl oz (30ml) sunflower oil	2 tablespoonsful sunflower oil
2-3 sweet red and green peppers, de-seeded and chopped	2-3 sweet red and green peppers, de-seeded and chopped
½ lb (225g) ripe tomatoes, skinned and chopped	8 ounces ripe tomatoes, skinned and chopped
2 teaspoonsful paprika	2 teaspoonsful paprika
Sea salt and freshly ground black pepper	Sea salt and freshly ground black pepper
4 eggs, beaten	4 eggs, beaten

1. Sauté the chopped onion in the oil until it is soft and transparent.

2. Add the peppers and the tomatoes and sprinkle with the paprika, salt and pepper. Cook until the peppers are soft.

3. Pour the beaten eggs over the vegetable mixture, and stir continuously until the eggs are cooked through.

4. Serve with brown rice.

ZIES EN ZOYER HOLISHKES
(Sweet and Sour Cabbage Rolls)

Imperial (Metric)	American
1 medium cabbage	1 medium cabbage
1 Klops recipe (pages 46-48)	1 Klops recipe (pages 46-48)
1 medium potato, grated	1 medium potato, grated
¾ pint (425ml) hot vegetable stock	2 cupsful hot vegetable stock
2 medium onions, grated	2 medium onions, grated
3 ripe tomatoes, skinned and chopped	3 ripe tomatoes, skinned and chopped
6 pitted prunes, cut into quarters	6 pitted prunes, cut into quarters
Sea salt and freshly ground black pepper	Sea salt and freshly ground black pepper
Juice of 1 medium lemon	Juice of 1 medium lemon
1½ tablespoonsful honey	1½ tablespoonsful honey

1. Place the cabbage in boiling, salted water for about 5 minutes, just long enough to soften leaves.

2. Separate leaves and wash carefully under running, cold water.

3. Mix grated potato into klops mixture. Moisten and soften with a little hot vegetable stock.

4. Place spoonsful of this mixture into the centre of each cabbage leaf and roll up carefully, closing the sides underneath the final fold, to prevent the filling from coming out.

5. Sauté the grated onions, together with leftover smaller cabbage leaves and place in the bottom of a greased ovenproof dish.

6. Arrange the cabbage rolls on top of this mixture.

7. Arrange the prunes and tomatoes on top of the rolls and season with salt and pepper.

8. Mix the lemon juice and honey with the vegetable stock and pour over the rolls (make sure that the rolls are not completely covered with the stock).

9. Cover with a lid and leave in the oven at 300°F/150°C (Gas Mark 2) for about 1½-2 hours, checking periodically to add more stock as required and basting. Brown with the lid off during the last 20 minutes. Add more honey or lemon juice if required. Serve with brown rice and salads.

GALUPTZI
(Spicy Cabbage Rolls)

Imperial (Metric)	American
1 medium cabbage	1 medium cabbage
1 Klops recipe (pages 46-48), moistened with a little hot vegetable stock	1 Klops recipe (pages 46-48), moistened with a little hot vegetable stock
2oz (55g) raw brown rice	5 tablespoonsful raw brown rice
1 tablespoonful parsley, chopped	1 tablespoonful parsley, chopped
1 clove garlic, crushed	1 clove garlic, crushed
1 teaspoonful yeast extract	1 teaspoonful yeast extract
1 teaspoonful mixed herbs	1 teaspoonful mixed herbs
Sea salt and freshly ground black pepper	Sea salt and freshly ground black pepper
Paprika, ginger and cinnamon	Paprika, ginger and cinnamon
2 ripe tomatoes, skinned and chopped	2 ripe tomatoes, skinned and chopped
1 onion, finely chopped	1 onion, finely chopped
¾ pint (425ml) vegetable stock, heated	2 cupsful vegetable stock, heated
Arrowroot or wholemeal flour, for thickening gravy	Arrowroot or wholewheat flour, for thickening gravy

1. Place the cabbage in boiling, salted water for about 5 minutes, just long enough to soften leaves. Separate the leaves and wash carefully under running, cold water.

2. Mix the raw brown rice into the klops mixture. Add all the seasonings and spices, the parsley and the yeast extract.

3. Place spoonsful of this mixture into the centre of each cabbage leaf and roll up carefully, closing the sides well.

4. Place the remaining cabbage leaves in well-greased ovenproof dish and place cabbage rolls on top. Add chopped tomatoes and onion and hot stock.

5. Cover with a lid and bake at 300°F/150°C (Gas Mark 2) for about 2 hours.

6. Baste periodically and add more stock if necessary. Brown during the last 20 minutes. Thicken the gravy with a little arrowroot or flour.

STUFFED AUBERGINES

Imperial (Metric)	American
4 medium aubergines	4 medium eggplants
2 medium onions, finely chopped	2 medium onions, finely chopped
2 cloves garlic, crushed	2 cloves garlic, crushed
3 tablespoonsful corn oil	3 tablespoonsful corn oil
Sea salt and freshly ground black pepper	Sea salt and freshly ground black pepper
1 teaspoonful paprika	1 teaspoonful paprika
2 tablespoonsful fresh parsley, chopped	2 tablespoonsful fresh parsley, chopped
3 soft, ripe tomatoes, skinned and chopped	3 soft, ripe tomatoes, skinned and chopped
½ lb (225g) Tvp, cooked in vegetable stock	1 cupful Tvp, cooked in vegetable stock

1. Slice the aubergines (eggplants) in half lengthwise, and sprinkle the cut sides with salt. Allow to rest for 30 minutes. Rinse well under running water.

2. Scoop out the pulp, leaving a little to support the skins.

3. Sauté the onions and garlic in the oil until soft. Fry the aubergine (eggplant) skins for 5 minutes to soften. Remove from pan.

4. Add the seasoning and the paprika, then the aubergine (eggplant) pulp, parsley and tomatoes. Cook until everything is soft.

5. Combine with the Tvp, mixing very well.

6. Fill the aubergine (eggplant) skins with the mixture.

7. Place them close together on an oiled ovenproof dish. Dot with margarine.

8. Bake at 350°F/180°C (Gas Mark 4) for about 30-40 minutes. Serve with brown rice, vegetables and salads.

KISHIM MIMULAIM
(Stuffed Courgettes)

Imperial (Metric)	American
4-6 courgettes	4-6 zucchini
½ recipe for Klops (pages 46-48) moistened with a little hot vegetable stock	½ recipe Klops (pages 46-48), moistened with a little hot vegetable stock
2 large ripe tomatoes, peeled and chopped	2 large ripe tomatoes, peeled and chopped
Sea salt and freshly ground black pepper	Sea salt and freshly ground black pepper
Paprika	Paprika
½ teaspoonful Demerara sugar	½ teaspoonful Demerara sugar
Vegetable stock *or* water, heated	Vegetable stock *or* water, heated

1. Wash the courgettes (zucchini) well and cut in half lengthwise. Scrape out the pulp and reserve.

2. Fill the hollows with the klops mixture.

3. Put the pulp in the bottom of a casserole dish and place the stuffed vegetables on top of this pulp.

4. Add the chopped tomatoes, seasonings and sugar, scattering these in between the stuffed vegetables.

5. Add a little hot vegetable stock or water, but not sufficient to cover the vegetables.

6. Bake, covered, at 325°F/170°C (Gas Mark 3) for about 45 minutes. Uncover to allow to brown for about 15 minutes. Serve with brown rice and salads.

TOMATES REYANADOS
(Baked Stuffed Tomatoes)

Imperial (Metric)	American
4oz (115g) Tvp mince	1 cupful Tvp mince
1 onion, finely chopped	1 onion, finely chopped
1 clove garlic, crushed	1 clove garlic, crushed
1 tablespoonful tomato purée	1 tablespoonful tomato paste
1 teaspoonful yeast extract	1 teaspoonful yeast extract
2 tablespoonsful chopped parsley	2 tablespoonsful chopped parsley
2 tablespoonsful soft wholemeal breadcrumbs	2 tablespoonsful soft wholewheat breadcrumbs
2 eggs	2 eggs
Sea salt and freshly ground black pepper	Sea salt and freshly ground black pepper
4 firm, large tomatoes	4 firm, large tomatoes
2 tablespoonsful wholemeal flour	2 tablespoonsful wholewheat flour
1 fl oz (30ml) sunflower oil	2 tablespoonsful sunflower oil
1 teaspoonful Demerara sugar	1 teaspoonful Demerara sugar

1. Hydrate the Tvp according to package instructions.

2. Lightly fry the chopped onion and crushed garlic and add to hydrated Tvp, together with tomato purée (paste) and yeast extract. Mix well.

3. Add the chopped parsley, breadcrumbs, one of the eggs, sea salt and black pepper and mix everything well together.

4. Cut each tomato in half and scoop out the pulp. Reserve the pulp.

5. Fill with the Tvp mixture. If there is any Tvp mixture over, form into little balls.

6. Beat the remaining egg, and dip the tomatoes, filled side down into the egg and then into the seasoned wholemeal flour. The little Tvp mixture balls may also be dipped in the same way.

7. Fry for a few minutes, cut side down, in a little oil.

8. Arrange, filled side up, with the Tvp balls, in greased ovenproof casserole. Pour over the mashed tomato pulp mixed with the sugar, parsley and a little hot water or vegetable stock.

9. Bake, covered, at 350°F/180° (Gas Mark 4) for about 20 minutes. Uncover for the last 10-15 minutes. Serve with brown rice and a green salad.

Note: If you prefer, you may use continental brown lentils instead of the Tvp mince as a filling. In that case, soak 6oz (170g/1 cupful) lentils overnight, and rinse well and cook for about 1 hour until soft. Mash well or purée and proceed with the recipe. You may need to add a few tablespoonsful of hot water or stock to soften and moisten the mixture.

LAHNE BE SAHEM
(Layered Casserole)

Imperial (Metric)	American
4oz (115g) Tvp mince	1 cupful Tvp mince
1 tablespoonful tomato purée	1 tablespoonful tomato paste
1 teaspoonful yeast extract	1 teaspoonful yeast extract
3 large onions, sliced	3 large onions, sliced
1 clove garlic, crushed	1 clove garlic, crushed
1 large green pepper, sliced and de-seeded (optional)	1 large green pepper, sliced and de-seeded (optional)
3 tablespoonsful sunflower oil	3 tablespoonsful sunflower oil
4-5 ripe tomatoes, sliced	4-5 ripe tomatoes, sliced
6 parboiled potatoes, sliced	6 parboiled potatoes, sliced
Juice of 1 lemon	Juice of 1 lemon
2 tablespoonsful chopped parsley	2 tablespoonsful chopped parsley
Sea salt and freshly ground black pepper	Sea salt and freshly ground black pepper

1. Hydrate Tvp according to package instructions. Add tomato purée (paste) and yeast extract and mix in well.

2. Lightly fry the sliced onions, garlic and green pepper in the oil until they are soft.

3. Drain the onions, garlic and green pepper and reserve the oil.

4. Arrange alternating layers of onions and green peppers, tomatoes, potatoes and Tvp mince in an ovenproof casserole.

5. Combine the oil in which the onions and green peppers were fried with the lemon juice, the parsley and a little sea salt and freshly ground black pepper. Pour over the casserole mixture with a little hot water.

6. Bake at 350°F/180°C (Gas Mark 4) for about 30-40 minutes.

Variation:
Substitute cooked, mashed continental lentils for the Tvp mince.

CHOLENT AND KNAIDEL
(Bean and Barley Casserole with Dumplings)

For the cholent:

Imperial (Metric)	American
1 large onion, chopped up finely	1 large onion, chopped up finely
Vegetable oil	Vegetable oil
9oz (260g) butter beans, soaked overnight and rinsed well	1½ cupsful Lima beans, soaked overnight and rinsed well
½lb (225g) barley, well rinsed	1 cupful barley, well rinsed
½oz (15g) wholemeal flour	2 tablespoonsful wholewheat flour
1 teaspoonful paprika	1 teaspoonful paprika
Sea salt, freshly ground black pepper and garlic salt	Sea salt, freshly ground black pepper and garlic salt
2 large potatoes, peeled and thickly sliced	2 large potatoes, peeled and thickly sliced
Hot vegetable stock to cover	Hot vegetable stock to cover

1. Fry the chopped onion in a little oil until golden-brown.

2. Place the onion, beans and barley in the bottom of an ovenproof casserole which should have a tightly fitting lid.

3. Mix together the flour and seasonings and add to the casserole, covering the beans, barley and onions and mixing in well.

4. Cover with thickly sliced potatoes, season with salt and pepper.

5. Pour sufficient hot vegetable stock into casserole to cover everything.

6. Cover with a lid and cook in the oven at 350°F/180°C (Gas Mark 4) for about 45 minutes. Meanwhile make the knaidels.

For the knaidels (dumplings):

Imperial (Metric)	American
4oz (115g) wholemeal flour	1 cupful wholewheat flour
2oz (55g) wholemeal semolina	½ cupful wholewheat semolina
Sea salt and freshly ground black pepper	Sea salt and freshly ground black pepper
3oz (85g) polyunsaturated margarine	⅓ cupful polyunsaturated margarine
2 tablespoonsful grated onion, lightly sautéed in oil	2 tablespoonsful grated onion, lightly sautéed in oil
1 finely grated potato	1 finely grated potato
1 teaspoonful chopped parsley	1 teaspoonful chopped parsley
1 egg (optional)	1 egg (optional)
1 teaspoonful yeast extract	1 teaspoonful yeast extract
2 fl oz (60ml) cold water	4 tablespoonsful cold water

1. Combine the flour, semolina and seasonings and rub in the margarine.

2. Add the sautéd onion, grated potato, parsley, egg (if using), yeast extract and enough of the cold water to make a soft mixture.

3. Form into dumplings about the size of golf balls.

4. Remove the casserole from the oven and place dumplings on top of the mixture.

5. Add more hot vegetable stock up to the level of the dumplings. Replace lid.

6. Leave in a slow oven 250°F/130°C (Gas Mark ½) overnight, or all day until required.

7. Cholent is traditionally served with Tzimmes (page 78).

Note: The types of beans used may be varied according to preference. (Red kidney beans MUST BE BOILED FIERCELY FOR AT LEAST 10 MINUTES before being placed in a slow cooking casserole.)

BOBOTIE

Imperial (Metric)	American
½ lb (225g) Tvp mince	2 cupsful Tvp mince
1 slice wholemeal bread	1 slice wholewheat bread
⅓ pint (200ml) milk	¾ cupful milk
1 onion, finely chopped	1 onion, finely chopped
1 fl oz (30ml) corn oil	2 tablespoonsful corn oil
1 tablespoonful curry powder	1 tablespoonful curry powder
1 tablespoonful tomato purée	1 tablespoonful tomato paste
2 teaspoonsful Demerara sugar	2 teaspoonsful Demerara sugar
1 tablespoonful cider vinegar	1 tablespoonful cider vinegar
Sea salt and freshly ground black pepper	Sea salt and freshly ground black pepper
1 teaspoonful mixed dried herbs	1 teaspoonful mixed dried herbs
2 eggs	2 eggs
1 oz (30g) chopped almonds	¼ cupful chopped almonds

1. Hydrate the Tvp mince according to package directions.

2. Soak the bread in a little of the milk and then mash well with a fork.

3. Sauté the onion in the oil until golden-brown.

4. Add the curry powder, tomato purée, (paste) sugar, vinegar, seasonings and herbs to the onion, stir well and cook for a few minutes.

5. Combine with the hydrated Tvp mince, the mashed bread and one of the eggs, beaten.

6. Place in greased casserole dish and cook in the oven at 350°F/180°C (Gas Mark 4) for about 30 minutes.

7. Beat the second egg very well with the rest of the milk and season with a little sea salt and ground black pepper and pour over the Tvp mince mixture.

8. Sprinkle with the chopped almonds and return to the oven for about 20-30 minutes. Serve with brown rice and salads.

Variation:
Substitute cooked, mashed continental lentils for the Tvp mince.

SOYA BEAN GOULASH

Imperial (Metric)	American
1 onion, chopped	1 onion, chopped
1 green pepper, de-seeded and chopped	1 green pepper, de-seeded and chopped
3 tablespoonsful corn oil	3 tablespoonsful corn oil
1 tablespoonful paprika	1 tablespoonful paprika
1 tablespoonful caraway seeds	1 tablespoonful caraway seeds
Garlic salt	Garlic salt
1 ripe tomato, skinned and chopped	1 ripe tomato, skinned and chopped
2 tablespoonsful tomato purée	2 tablespoonsful tomato paste
1 teaspoonful yeast extract	1 teaspoonful yeast extract
1 tablespoonful chopped parsley	1 tablespoonful chopped parsley
4oz (115g) mushrooms, chopped	2 cupsful mushrooms, chopped
½lb (225g) cooked soya beans	1 cupful cooked soy beans
Sea salt and freshly ground black pepper	Sea salt and freshly ground black pepper
¾ pint (425ml) hot vegetable stock	2 cupsful hot vegetable stock
3-4 parboiled potatoes	3-4 parboiled potatoes

1. Sauté the onion and green pepper until they are soft.

2. Stir in the paprika, caraway seeds and garlic salt, and sauté for another 5 minutes.

3. Add the tomato, tomato purée, (paste) yeast extract, parsley and mushrooms and cook for about 10 minutes.

4. Transfer to an ovenproof casserole which has a lid.

5. Add the beans, sea salt and black pepper and the hot stock.

6. Leave in a slow oven 300°F/150°C (Gas Mark 2) for 2-2½ hours.

7. About 1 hour before serving, add the potatoes. Serve with brown rice and salad.

Note: Dry soya beans may be placed in water and kept in the refrigerator for 3 days, changing the water and rinsing well every day. They may then be brought to the boil, rinsed well, and cooked for 2-3 hours until ready for use. Those not wanted immediately may be frozen and kept for later use.

ARROZ ASAPADO
(Chick Pea and Rice Casserole)

Imperial (Metric)	American
½ lb (225g) chick peas, pre-cooked	1 cupful garbanzo beans, pre-cooked
2 large onions, finely chopped	2 large onions, finely chopped
2 cloves garlic, crushed	2 cloves garlic, crushed
2 fl oz (60ml) vegetable oil	¼ cupful vegetable oil
2 large, ripe tomatoes, skinned and chopped	2 large, ripe tomatoes, skinned and chopped
Sea salt and freshly ground black pepper	Sea salt and freshly ground black pepper
1⅓ pints (770ml) hot vegetable stock	3¼ cupsful hot vegetable stock
½ lb (225g) brown rice	1 cupful brown rice

1. Chick peas (garbanzo beans) should be soaked in cold water and kept in the refrigerator for 24 hours. They should be thoroughly rinsed, then brought to the boil for 10 minutes, rinsed again, and re-cooked until soft (about 2-3 hours simmering).

2. Gently fry the onions and garlic in the oil until they are golden-brown.

3. Add the tomatoes and seasonings and simmer for about 5 minutes.

4. Add the hot stock, rice and chick peas (garbanzo beans).

5. Bring to the boil, then turn down heat and simmer for about 30 minutes until the liquid has been absorbed and the rice is cooked through.

6. Serve hot with accompanying vegetables of your choice.

Variation:

For extra interest, add 2-3oz (55-85g/1 cupful) fresh mushrooms and a few tablespoonsful of chopped green pepper, which should be fried with the onions and garlic.

MEJEDRA
(Rice and Lentil Pilaff)

Imperial (Metric)	American
½ lb (225g) brown rice	1 cupful brown rice
Sea salt	Sea salt
1 teaspoonful mixed dried herbs	1 teaspoonful mixed dried herbs
Hot vegetable stock	Hot vegetable stock
3 onions, thinly sliced	3 onions, thinly sliced
1 fl oz (30ml) sunflower oil, or slightly more if needed	2 tablespoonsful sunflower oil, or slightly more if needed
2 oz (55g) blanched, chopped almonds	½ cupful blanched, chopped almonds
2 tablespoonsful raisins	2½ tablespoonsful raisins
½ lb (225g) continental (brown) lentils, soaked overnight	1 cupful continental (brown) lentils, soaked overnight
Freshly ground black pepper	Freshly ground black pepper

1. Place the rinsed rice in a pan with 1 teaspoonful sea salt, half the dried herbs and 2½ times its volume of hot vegetable stock. Bring to the boil, then simmer gently until all the stock is absorbed (about 30 minutes). Set aside.

2. Sauté two onions in the oil until they are golden-brown.

3. Add the chopped nuts and fry gently for a few minutes.

4. Rinse the raisins under hot running water and add to the onion and nut mixture. Set this mixture aside.

5. Gently fry the remaining onion in a little oil in a saucepan, add the lentils, the rest of the herbs and enough vegetable stock to cover.

6. Bring to the boil and simmer until the lentils are soft (about 1 hour).

7. Combine the cooked rice and lentils, add a little hot stock, sea salt and black pepper and bring to the boil again.

8. Simmer on very slow heat until all the liquid has been absorbed. Serve with the onion, almond and raisin mixture piled on top.

BOREKAS

For the filling:

Imperial (Metric)	American
2 eggs, beaten	2 eggs, beaten
½ lb (225g) cooked, chopped spinach	1 cupful cooked, chopped spinach
4oz (115g) grated yellow cheese *or* curd cheese	1 cupful grated yellow cheese *or* ½ cupful curd cheese
Sea salt and freshly ground black pepper	Sea salt and freshly ground black pepper

1. Reserve some of the beaten egg for topping.

2. Combine the rest of the ingredients and mix thoroughly.

For the pastry:

Imperial (Metric)	American
½ lb (225g) 81 per cent wholemeal flour	2 cupsful 81 per cent wholewheat flour
Sea salt and freshly ground black pepper	Sea salt and freshly ground black pepper
2 teaspoonsful baking powder	2 teaspoonsful baking powder
1 egg	1 egg
2 fl oz (60ml) sunflower oil	¼ cupful sunflower oil
Water to mix to a soft dough	Water to mix to a soft dough
Sesame seeds	Sesame seeds

1. Sift together the flour, seasoning and baking powder, tipping back the bran.

2. Make a well in the flour and add the lightly-beaten egg and the oil.

3. Mix with a wooden-spoon to form a dough, adding as much water as needed to make the dough soft and pliable.

4. Knead and roll out the dough thinly and cut into squares, about 4 inches (10cm) or smaller.

5. Put a tablespoonful of filling into each square and fold over to form a triangle. Pinch the edges together with moistened fingers to seal.

6. Brush with the reserved beaten egg and sprinkle with sesame seeds.

7. Bake in a well-greased baking tray for about 30 minutes until golden-brown, at 350°F/180°C (Gas Mark 4).

4. Side Dishes

FRITADA DE ESPINACA
(Spinach Soufflé)

Imperial (Metric)	American
1 lb (450g) cooked *or* defrosted spinach plus liquid	2 cupsful cooked *or* defrosted spinach plus liquid
4 oz (115g) grated cheese	1 cupful grated cheese
3 eggs, well beaten	3 eggs, well beaten
1 oz (30g) soft wholemeal breadcrumbs	½ cupful soft wholemeal breadcrumbs
¼ pint (140ml) milk	⅔ cupful milk
Sea salt and freshly ground black pepper	Sea salt and freshly ground black pepper

1. Combine all the ingredients together and mix well.

2. Place in well-greased casserole.

3. Bake at 350°F/180°C (Gas Mark 4) for about 30 minutes or until golden brown.

ONIONS WITH FRUIT

Imperial (Metric)	American
1 tablespoonful tomato purée	1 tablespoonful tomato paste
2 tablespoonsful sunflower oil	2 tablespoonsful sunflower oil
Juice of 1 lemon	Juice of 1 lemon
2 teaspoonsful honey	2 teaspoonsful honey
¼ pint (140ml) water	⅔ cupful water
Sea salt and freshly ground black pepper	Sea salt and freshly ground black pepper
1 lb (450g) small onions	1 pound small onions
4 dried pears *or* 1 fresh pear	4 dried pears *or* 1 fresh pear
6 dried prunes	6 dried prunes
6 dried apricots	6 dried apricots

1. Mix the tomato purée, (paste) oil, lemon juice, honey and water together and bring to the boil. Add a pinch of salt and pepper.

2. Add the onions, cover saucepan and simmer for about 10 minutes.

3. If using fresh pear, peel and slice into 8 segments.

4. Transfer to an ovenproof dish, add the dried prunes, apricots and pear pieces. Add a little more water if needed.

5. Bake at 325°F/170°C (Gas Mark 3) for about 40 minutes.

6. Makes a delicious accompaniment to Klops (pages 46-48) or Koklaten (pages 49-51).

CREAMED BEETROOT

Imperial (Metric)	American
4 or 5 medium beetroot	4 or 5 medium beets
1 oz (30g) polyunsaturated margarine	2½ tablespoonsful polyunsaturated margarine
1 oz (30g) 81 per cent wholemeal flour	2 tablespoonsful 81 per cent wholewheat flour
Approximately ½ pint (285ml) cooking water from beetroot	Approximately 1½ cupsful cooking water from beets
2 teaspoonsful Demerara sugar	2 teaspoonsful Demerara sugar
2 teaspoonsful lemon juice	2 teaspoonsful lemon juice
Sea salt and freshly ground black pepper	Sea salt and freshly ground black pepper

1. Wash beetroot (beets) well, peel and boil until tender. Cut into small pieces.

2. Melt the margarine, remove from heat and blend in the flour.

3. Add liquid from the cooked beetroot (beet) and stir over the heat until it thickens.

4. Add the sugar, lemon juice, salt and pepper. Cook for a few minutes. Pour over the beetroot (beet) pieces and serve hot.

VIENNESE BEETROOT

Imperial (Metric)	American
4 or 5 medium beetroot	4 or 5 medium beets
1 oz (30g) soft wholemeal breadcrumbs	½ cupful soft wholemeal breadcrumbs
1 egg, beaten	1 egg, beaten
1 pint (285ml) milk	2½ cupsful milk
Sea salt and freshly ground black pepper	Sea salt and freshly ground black pepper
1 oz (30g) polyunsaturated margarine	2½ tablespoonsful polyunsaturated margarine

1. Wash beetroot (beets) very well to remove any soil. Do not peel, and leave the root on to avoid too much loss of juice. Boil until tender. Peel and cut into slices.

2. Place in a greased casserole, with breadcrumbs sprinkled between each layer.

3. Sprinkle breadcrumbs over the top layer and dot with margarine.

4. Mix the beaten egg with the milk and add sea salt and black pepper. Pour over the beetroot (beets).

5. Bake at 325°F/170°C (Gas Mark 3) until browned. Serve hot.

TZIMMES

Imperial (Metric)	American
2 medium onions, finely chopped	2 medium onions, finely chopped
2 cloves garlic, crushed	2 cloves garlic, crushed
2 tablespoonsful sunflower oil	2 tablespoonsful sunflower oil
1 lb (450g) carrots, grated	1 pound carrots, grated
2 tablespoonsful ground almonds	2 tablespoonsful ground almonds
1 egg	1 egg
¼ teaspoonful freshly ground black pepper	¼ teaspoonful freshly ground black pepper
1 teaspoonful lemon juice	1 teaspoonful lemon juice
2-3 oz (55-85g) fresh wholemeal breadcrumbs	1-1½ cupsful fresh wholewheat breadcrumbs

1. Sauté the chopped onions and garlic in oil until soft and golden.

2. Add the grated carrots, cook and stir for 5 minutes.

3. Remove from the heat.

4. Combine with the rest of the ingredients, adding just enough breadcrumbs to make a firm consistency.

5. Bake in a greased ovenproof casserole at 400°F/200°C (Gas Mark 6) for about 30 minutes.

COURGETTES AND TOMATOES

Imperial (Metric)	American
1 large onion, chopped	1 large onion, chopped
2 cloves garlic, crushed	2 cloves garlic, crushed
2 tablespoonsful chopped green pepper	2 tablespoonsful chopped green pepper
2 tablespoonsful corn oil	2 tablespoonsful corn oil
Sea salt and freshly ground black pepper	Sea salt and freshly ground black pepper
1 tablespoonful fresh parsley, chopped	1 tablespoonful fresh parsley, chopped
3 large, ripe tomatoes, skinned and chopped	3 large, ripe tomatoes, skinned and chopped
¼ teaspoonful dried oregano	¼ teaspoonful dried oregano
4-5 courgettes, sliced, unpeeled	4-5 zucchini, sliced, unpeeled

1. Sauté the onion, garlic and green pepper in the oil until soft.

2. Add the seasonings, herbs and chopped tomatoes and cook over a low heat for about 5 minutes.

3. To this mixture, add the courgettes (zucchini) and cook gently until they are soft (about 20 minutes).

CRUMBED CAULIFLOWER

Imperial (Metric)	American
1 cauliflower	1 cauliflower
2oz (55g) dried wholemeal breadcrumbs	½ cupful dried wholewheat breadcrumbs
Sea salt and freshly ground black pepper	Sea salt and freshly ground black pepper
½ teaspoonful mixed dried herbs	½ teaspoonful mixed dried herbs
2 tablespoonsful coarsely chopped nuts	2 tablespoonsful coarsely chopped nuts
2oz (55g) butter or polyunsaturated margarine	¼ cupful butter or polyunsaturated margarine

1. Wash the cauliflower well in salted water.

2. Divide into florets and boil in a little water or steam until tender. Place in an ovenproof casserole.

3. Mix dried breadcrumbs, salt, pepper, herbs and nuts together and sprinkle over cauliflower florets.

4. Dab with the butter or margarine. Brown in the oven at 375°F/190°C (Gas Mark 5) for about 10-15 minutes.

POTATO KUGEL

Imperial (Metric)	American
4-6 medium potatoes	4-6 medium potatoes
1 small onion	1 small onion
1oz (30g) butter or polyunsaturated margarine	2½ tablespoonsful butter or polyunsaturated margarine
2 eggs, beaten	2 eggs, beaten
2 tablespoonsful wholemeal flour	2 tablespoonsful wholewheat flour
1 teaspoonful sea salt	1 teaspoonful sea salt
1 teaspoonful baking powder	1 teaspoonful baking powder

1. Grate the potatoes and onion finely.

2. Melt the butter or margarine in an ovenproof casserole and mix in the grated potatoes and onion.

3. Add all the other ingredients and mix well.

4. Bake at 350°F/180°C (Gas Mark 4) until golden-brown and firm (about 30-40 minutes).

SWEET AND SOUR CABBAGE

Imperial (Metric)	American
1 onion, chopped	1 onion, chopped
1 fl oz (30ml) sunflower oil	2 tablespoonsful sunflower oil
1 lb (450g) red cabbage, shredded	4 cupsful shredded red cabbage
1 large apple, grated	1 large apple, grated
2 fl oz (60ml) vegetable stock	1/4 cupful vegetable stock
Sea salt and freshly ground black pepper	Sea salt and freshly ground black pepper
Juice of 1/2 lemon	Juice of 1/2 lemon
2 teaspoonsful honey	2 teaspoonsful honey
2 tablespoonsful sweet red wine (optional)	2 tablespoonsful sweet red wine (optional)

1. Sauté the onion in oil for a few minutes.

2. Add the cabbage, the apple, stock, seasonings, lemon juice and honey and cook gently for about 15 minutes.

3. Add the wine, if using, and place in an ovenproof casserole with a lid.

4. Bake at 350°F/180°C (Gas Mark 4) for about 1 to 1½ hours.

FASOULIA
(Sephardic Green Beans)

Imperial (Metric)	American
1 lb (450g) French *or* runner beans, fresh	1 pound snap *or* young green beans, fresh
1 small onion, finely chopped	1 small onion, finely chopped
1 clove garlic, crushed	1 clove garlic, crushed
2 tablespoonsful sunflower oil	2 tablespoonsful sunflower oil
2-3 large, ripe tomatoes, skinned and chopped	2-3 large, ripe tomatoes, skinned and chopped
Sea salt and freshly ground black pepper	Sea salt and freshly ground black pepper
4 fl oz (120ml) hot water	½ cupful hot water

1. Wash and prepare the beans by topping and tailing them and cutting them into slices.

2. Lightly fry the onions and garlic in the oil for a few minutes, then add the beans, tomatoes, seasoning and water.

3. Cook, covered, at 350°F/180°C (Gas Mark 4) or simmer on top of the cooker for 20-30 minutes, until beans are tender.

CARROT AND POTATO TZIMMES

Imperial (Metric)	American
1 lb (450g) fresh carrots	1 pound fresh carrots
2 parsnips	2 parsnips
2-3 large potatoes	2-3 large potatoes
1 small onion, quartered	1 small onion, quartered
2 oz (55g) shredded cabbage	½ cupful shredded cabbage
2 tablespoonsful sunflower seed oil	2 tablespoonsful sunflower seed oil
7 fl oz (200ml) hot vegetable stock	¾ cupful hot vegetable stock
2 teaspoonsful 81 per cent wholemeal flour	2 teaspoonsful 81 per cent wholewheat flour
2 teaspoonsful Demerara sugar	2 teaspoonsful Demerara sugar
Sea salt and freshly ground black pepper	Sea salt and freshly ground black pepper
8-10 prunes, soaked and cut into halves (plus liquid)	8-10 prunes, soaked and cut into halves (plus liquid)

1. Clean and prepare the root vegetables and cut into chunks.

2. Lightly fry the onion and cabbage in the oil until soft and transfer to an ovenproof casserole with lid.

3. Cook the root vegetables in the stock over low heat for about 10 minutes and transfer to the casserole.

4. Mix the flour, sugar, salt and pepper with a little cold water to form a creamy liquid. Slowly add the stock in which the vegetables were cooking and pour over the vegetables in casserole.

5. Place the prune halves amongst the vegetables and add the prune liquid.

6. Cover and bake at 325°F/170°C (Gas Mark 3) for about 45 minutes, until all vegetables are tender. Add more water or stock if necessary.

7. Uncover and brown for about another 30 minutes.

LATKES
(Potato Fritters)

Imperial (Metric)	American
1 lb (450g) potatoes	1 pound potatoes
1 medium onion	1 medium onion
2 eggs	2 eggs
1 teaspoonful sea salt	1 teaspoonful sea salt
Freshly ground black pepper	Freshly ground black pepper
1 teaspoonful light Demerara sugar	1 teaspoonful light Demerara sugar
1 oz (30g) wholemeal flour	1/4 cupful wholewheat flour
1 teaspoonful baking powder	1 teaspoonful baking powder
Vegetable oil for frying	Vegetable oil for frying

1. Peel the potatoes thinly. Grate the potatoes and onion, but not too coarsely.

2. Beat the eggs until frothy and add to the grated mixture, together with the seasonings and sugar.

3. Stir the flour and baking powder together and add to the potato mixture.

4. Heat the oil in a frying pan (not too much) and drop tablespoonsful of the mixture into the hot oil.

5. Fry on both sides until golden brown.

6. Keep warm in the oven and serve warm.

5. Salads

KIBBUTZ SALAD

Imperial (Metric)	American
3 firm, ripe tomatoes	3 firm, ripe tomatoes
1 medium, green pepper	1 medium, green pepper
½·1 cucumber	½·1 cucumber

1. Wash the tomatoes and cut into small bite-sized pieces.

2. Wash the green pepper and remove seeds. Chop finely.

3. Wash, but do not peel, the cucumber and cut into bite-sized pieces.

4. Mix all the ingredients together.

5. Serve with tahini dressing (obtainable in most health food shops) or with Simple Salad Dressing (page 89).

LENTIL SALAD

Imperial (Metric)	American
10oz (280g) continental (brown) lentils	1½ cupsful continental (brown) lentils
Simple Salad Dressing (page 89) made with olive oil or sunflower oil and lemon juice	Simple Salad Dressing (page 89) made with olive oil or sunflower oil and lemon juice
Sea salt and freshly ground black pepper	Sea salt and freshly ground black pepper
1 small spring onion, finely chopped	1 small scallion, finely chopped

1. Rinse the lentils well under running cold water and soak overnight in cold water in the refrigerator. Rinse again under running cold water.

2. Cover with cold water, bring to the boil and simmer gently for about 1 hour until lentils are tender. Strain and reserve any remaining liquid for use as stock in other dishes.

3. Liberally sprinkle the hot lentils with salad dressing. Season to taste with sea salt and ground black pepper.

4. Serve cold, mixing in the chopped onions and more salad dressing.

SPINACH SALAD

Imperial (Metric)	American
1 lb (450g) fresh spinach leaves	1 pound fresh spinach leaves
2 oz (55g) fresh white mushrooms	1 cupful fresh white mushrooms
2 small spring onions	2 small scallions
1 hard-boiled egg (optional)	1 hard-boiled egg (optional)
Garlic-flavoured wholemeal croûtons (optional)	Garlic-flavoured wholewheat croûtons (optional)

1. Wash the spinach leaves very well under cold running water and inspect carefully for insects. Tear into small pieces and place in a salad bowl.

2. Wash the mushrooms very carefully and slice thinly.

3. Wash and finely chop the spring onions (scallions).

4. Mash the hard-boiled egg, if using.

5. Scatter sliced mushrooms, chopped onions and hard-boiled egg over spinach leaves, also croûtons if using. Serve with Simple Salad Dressing (page 89).

Note: To make the croûtons, cut 2 slices of bread into small pieces (the size of a pea) and fry lightly in vegetable oil until golden. Add sliced garlic and ¼ teaspoonful mixed herbs to the frying oil.

PICKLED CUCUMBER SALAD

Imperial (Metric)	American
2 large cucumbers *or* 4-5 small cucumbers	2 large cucumbers *or* 4-5 small cucumbers
2 cloves garlic, sliced	2 cloves garlic, sliced
⅔ pint (340ml) cider vinegar	1½ cupsful cider vinegar
4 fl oz (120ml) cold water	½ cupful cold water
2 oz (55g) Demerara sugar or less	⅓ cupful Demerara sugar or less
1 teaspoonful dill seed (optional)	1 teaspoonful dill seed (optional)
1 teaspoonful sea salt	1 teaspoonful sea salt
Freshly ground black pepper	Freshly ground black pepper

1. Wash the cucumbers well, but do not peel. Cut into slices.

2. Boil together the vinegar, water, sugar, salt, garlic and pepper.

3. Add the sliced cucumbers and boil for just a few minutes. Remove from the heat.

4. Allow to cool and refrigerate in jar with dill seed if using. Serve cold as required.

CABBAGE AND CARROT SALAD

Imperial (Metric)	American
6oz (170g) grated carrots	1 cupful grated carrots
½lb (225g) shredded cabbage	2 cupsful shredded cabbage
1 spring onion, finely chopped	1 scallion, finely chopped
A few lettuce leaves, shredded	A few lettuce leaves, shredded
2 tablespoonsful chopped almonds	2 tablespoonsful chopped almonds
2 tablespoonsful raisins	2 tablespoonsful raisins
2½ tablespoonsful sunflower oil	2½ tablespoonsful sunflower oil
Juice of ½ lemon	Juice of ½ lemon
Celery salt	Celery salt
Sea salt and freshly ground black pepper	Sea salt and freshly ground black pepper
Orange slices for decoration	Orange slices for decoration

1. Combine the grated carrots, cabbage, spring onion (scallion), lettuce leaves, nuts and raisins, mixing well.

2. Mix the oil and lemon juice with a little water and celery salt and pepper, and pour over the salad.

3. Decorate with slices of orange.

4. Serve cold.

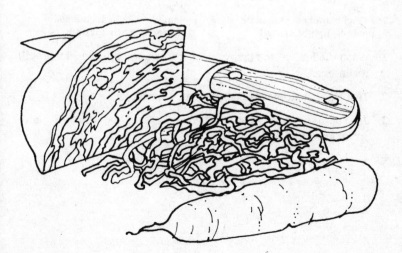

APPLE SALAD

Imperial (Metric)	American
4 juicy, red eating apples	4 juicy, red eating apples
Juice of ½ lemon	Juice of ½ lemon
Apple or orange juice	Apple or orange juice
2oz (55g) grapes	2 ounces grapes
1 large, sweet orange	1 large, sweet orange
1 celery stick	1 celery stalk
2 tablespoonsful chopped walnuts	2 tablespoonsful chopped English walnuts

1. Wash very well and dry, but do not peel, the apples. Cut into small pieces and place in a bowl. Squeeze lemon juice and a little apple or orange juice over apples to prevent discolouring.

2. Wash the grapes, cut each one in half and remove the pips.

3. Peel the orange and cut into small pieces.

4. Wash and finely chop the celery.

5. Mix everything together, chill and serve sprinkled with walnuts.

LETTUCE AND ALMOND SALAD

Imperial (Metric)	American
1 head lettuce (any variety)	1 head lettuce (any variety)
A few leaves endive or chicory	A few leaves endive or chicory
Simple Salad Dressing (page 89)	Simple Salad Dressing (page 89)
Sea salt and freshly ground black pepper	Sea salt and freshly ground black pepper
2oz (55g) blanched, chopped almonds, lightly toasted	½ cupful, blanched, chopped almonds, lightly toasted

1. Wash the lettuce and endive or chicory thoroughly, checking well for insects.

2. Tear into small pieces and place in a bowl.

3. Just before serving, toss with salad dressing and seasoning and sprinkle with almonds.

TABOOLI

Imperial (Metric)	American
4oz cracked wheat (bulgur)	⅔ cupful cracked wheat (bulgur)
½ pint (285ml) boiling water	1⅓ cupsful boiling water
1 tomato, finely chopped	1 tomato, finely chopped
½ cupful fresh parsley, finely chopped	½ cupful fresh parsley, finely chopped
2 spring onions, finely chopped	2 scallions, finely chopped
¼ cupful fresh mint, finely chopped *or* 1 tablespoonful dried mint	¼ cupful fresh mint, finely chopped, *or* 1 tablespoonful dried mint
Juice of 1 lemon	Juice of 1 lemon
2 fl oz (60ml) olive oil	¼ cupful olive oil
Sea salt and freshly ground black pepper	Sea salt and freshly ground black pepper
Lettuce and tomato, for garnish	Lettuce and tomato, for garnish

1. Rinse the cracked wheat under cold running water.

2. Pour the boiling water over the wheat and let it soak for about 1 hour until the water is absorbed and the wheat is tender. Drain off and squeeze out excess water.

3. Mix together all the chopped ingredients and combine with the wheat, mixing well.

4. Blend together the oil, lemon juice, salt and pepper and pour over the salad.

5. Serve chilled on lettuce leaves, decorated with tomato slices.

SIMPLE SALAD DRESSING

Imperial (Metric)	American
3 fl oz (90ml) salad oil	⅓ cupful salad oil
2 tablespoonsful lemon juice *or* cider vinegar	2 tablespoonsful lemon juice *or* cider vinegar
¼ teaspoonful sea salt	¼ teaspoonful sea salt
Pinch freshly ground black pepper	Pinch freshly ground black pepper
Pinch mustard powder (optional)	Pinch mustard powder (optional)
2 teaspoonsful chopped parsley (optional)	2 teaspoonsful chopped parsley (optional)

1. Mix all the ingredients very well together.

2. Keeps well in the refrigerator, but add parsley only just before serving, in this case.

6. Desserts

DRIED FRUIT COMPOTE

Imperial (Metric)	American
1 lb (450g) dried mixed fruit (peaches, pears, prunes, apples etc.)	1 pound dried mixed fruit (peaches, pears, prunes, apples etc.)
⅔ pint (340ml) apple *or* orange juice	1½ cupsful apple *or* orange juice
1 oz (30g) light Demerara sugar	2 tablespoonsful light Demerara sugar
2 oranges	2 oranges
1 pink grapefruit	1 pink grapefruit
Cream *or* yogurt and chopped nuts for serving (optional)	Cream *or* yogurt and chopped nuts for serving (optional)

1. Soak the dried fruit overnight in the fruit juice and sugar in the refrigerator.

2. After soaking bring to the boil, then cook on a low heat for about 20-30 minutes. Test fruit for softness.

3. Peel and cut the oranges and grapefruit into small segments.

4. Combine with the dried fruit mixture after it is removed from the heat.

5. Serve cold with cream or yogurt and chopped nuts, if liked.

BAKED APPLES

Imperial (Metric)	American
4-6 medium eating apples	4-6 medium eating apples
3 tablespoonsful chopped nuts	3 tablespoonsful chopped nuts
1 tablespoonful chopped raisins	1 tablespoonful chopped raisins
½ teaspoonful powdered cinnamon	½ teaspoonful powdered cinnamon
4 teaspoonsful honey	4 teaspoonsful honey
Butter *or* polyunsaturated margarine	Butter *or* polyunsaturated margarine

1. Wash the apples, but do not peel. Cut off the tops and remove the cores. Place in an ovenproof casserole.

2. Combine the nuts, raisins and cinnamon and fill each apple with this mixture.

3. Place a little honey on top of each filled apple, topped by a knob of butter or margarine.

4. Pour a little water into the casserole (about ½-¾ cupful) and bake at 350°F/180°C (Gas Mark 4) for about 30-40 minutes.

5. Serve warm, with cream, yogurt or custard.

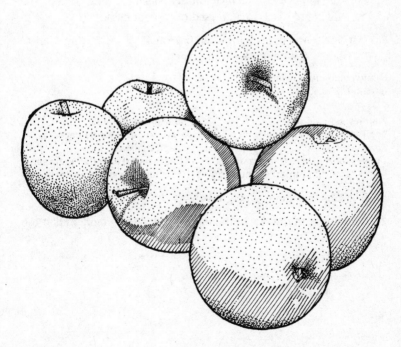

BLINTZES
(Stuffed Pancakes)

Batter:

Imperial (Metric)	American
3 eggs	3 eggs
¾ pint (425ml) mixed water and milk	2 cupsful mixed water and milk
6oz (170g) 81 per cent wholemeal flour	1½ cupsful 81 per cent wholewheat flour
½ teaspoonful baking powder	½ teaspoonful baking powder
Vegetable oil	Vegetable oil

1. Beat together the eggs and water and milk until frothy.

2. Gradually add the flour, sifted with the baking powder, beating the mixture until smooth.

3. Wipe a small frying pan (skillet) with kitchen paper dipped in a little vegetable oil and heat.

4. Pour sufficient batter into the pan to cover thinly and cook until done. Place on kitchen paper.

5. Repeat the process until all the batter has been used.

6. Fill each blintz with a tablespoonful of desired filling, roll up, fold the ends, and place in a greased ovenproof casserole.

7. Dot with butter or margarine and bake at 350°F/180°C (Gas Mark 4) for about 30-40 minutes until golden.

Coconut and Raisin Filling:

Imperial (Metric)	American
1 egg	1 egg
2 tablespoonsful milk	2 tablespoonsful milk
5oz (145g) desiccated coconut	1⅔ cupsful desiccated coconut
2oz (55g) raisins	⅓ cupful raisins
1 tablespoonful light Demerara sugar	1 tablespoonful light Demerara sugar
½ teaspoonful powdered cinnamon	½ teaspoonful powdered cinnamon

1. Beat together the egg and milk.

2. Combine with the rest of the ingredients, adding more milk if too dry.

Cheese Filling:

Imperial (Metric)	American
1 egg	1 egg
1-2 tablespoonsful creamy milk	1-2 tablespoonsful creamy milk
1 lb (450g) curd cheese	2 cupsful curd cheese
Sea salt	Sea salt
1-2 tablespoonsful light Demerara sugar	1-2 tablespoonsful light Demerara sugar

1. Beat together egg and milk and combine with all the other ingredients, mixing well.

2. Taste for desired sweetness, and add more milk if a moister filling is desired.

RUSSIAN BERRY KISSEL

Imperial (Metric)	American
1 lb (450g) mixed berries (strawberries, raspberries, blackberries or cherries)	1 pound mixed berries (strawberries, raspberries, blackberries or cherries)
¾ pint (425ml) water	2 cupsful water
2 oz (55g) Demerara sugar	⅓ cupsful Demerara sugar
2 teaspoonsful lemon juice	2 teaspoonsful lemon juice
1 tablespoonful blackcurrant juice	1 tablespoonful blackcurrant juice
2 tablespoonsful arrowroot	2 tablespoonsful arrowroot
2 tablespoonsful sweet red wine	2 tablespoonsful sweet red wine
Cream *or* yogurt and a few berries, for decoration	Cream *or* yogurt and a few berries, for decoration

1. Simmer the prepared and cleaned fruit in the water, sugar, lemon juice and blackcurrant juice until soft.

2. Purée the fruit by pressing through a sieve.

3. Mix the arrowroot with a little water and the wine to form a thin, creamy liquid.

4. Slowly add some of the hot fruit juice to this liquid, stirring all the time.

5. Combine the liquid with the puréed fruit and cook over a low heat, stirring until it thickens.

6. Serve cold, decorated with cream or yogurt and a few fresh berries.

TAPUZIM
(Orange Surprise)

Imperial (Metric)	American
½ pint (285ml) water	1⅓ cupsful water
3oz (85g) light Demerara sugar	½ cupful light Demerara sugar
4 large, sweet oranges	4 large, sweet oranges
1-2 tablespoonsful brandy *or* apricot liqueur	1-2 tablespoonsful brandy *or* apricot liqueur

1. Gently heat the water and sugar, and simmer for about 10 minutes.

2. Peel one orange very finely, taking care not to cut any of the white pith. Finely slice the peel and add it to the simmering syrup.

3. Peel the other three oranges, cutting away the pith. Cut the pith from the first orange.

4. Slice the oranges and remove any pips. Arrange in a dish.

5. Add the brandy or liqueur to the syrup and peel. Remove from the stove and pour over the sliced oranges. Turn the slices to keep them moist.

6. Serve chilled. Alternatively, this dish may be heated gently and served hot.

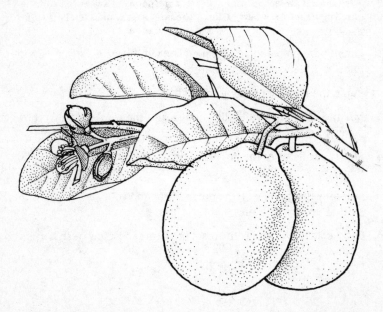

HUNGARIAN CHERRY CAKE

Imperial (Metric)	American
3 eggs	3 eggs
4oz (115g) light Demerara sugar	⅔ cupful light Demerara sugar
6oz (170g) polyunsaturated margarine *or* softened butter	⅔ cupful polyunsaturated margarine *or* softened butter
6oz (170g) 81 per cent wholemeal flour	1½ cupsful 81 per cent wholewheat flour
1lb (450g) sweet, red cherries (fresh or tinned)	1 pound sweet, red cherries (fresh or canned
Raw cane sugar	Raw cane sugar

1. Separate the egg yolks and whites.

2. Beat half the sugar with the 3 egg whites until stiff.

3. Cream the other half of the sugar with the margarine or butter. Beat in the egg yolks, a little at a time.

4. Fold the egg white mixture gently into the butter mixture.

5. Sift the flour to make it lighter and tip the bran back into it. Gently fold the flour into the mixture, a little at a time, using a metal spoon.

6. Pour the mixture into a greased, rectangular, paper-lined tin.

7. If using fresh cherries, de-pip them, if using tinned cherries, drain them. Press them into the batter.

8. Bake at 350°F/180°C (Gas Mark 4) for about 30 minutes, until golden-brown.

9. Sprinkle with a few teaspoonsful of raw cane sugar. Delicious warm or cold.

APPLE FARFEL TART

Pastry:

Imperial (Metric)	American
4oz (115g) butter *or* polyunsaturated margarine	½ cupful butter *or* polyunsaturated margarine
4oz (115g) light Demerara sugar	⅔ cupful light Demerara sugar
1 tablespoonful sunflower oil	1 tablespoonful sunflower oil
1 egg, beaten until frothy	1 egg, beaten until frothy
½ lb (225g) wholemeal flour	2 cupsful wholewheat flour
2 tablespoonsful ground nuts	2 tablespoonsful ground nuts

1. Cream the butter or margarine, sugar and oil together.

2. Add the beaten egg and mix well in.

3. Slowly add the flour and the ground nuts.

4. Knead lightly to make a soft but firm dough.

5. Take half the pastry and press into a greased pie dish, building up at the sides.

6. Reserve the other half of the pastry for the farfel topping.

Filling:

Imperial (Metric)	American
1 tablespoonful smooth apricot jam	1 tablespoonful smooth apricot jelly
1 tablespoonful Demerara sugar	1 tablespoonful Demerara sugar
1½ tablespoonsful water	1½ tablespoonful water
4 large eating apples, peeled and sliced thinly	4 large eating apples, peeled and sliced thinly

1. Make a syrup by combining the jam (jelly), sugar and water in a saucepan over a low heat.

2. Gently poach the prepared apples in the syrup until tender.

3. Drain the cooked apples and spread them over the pastry.

4. Grate the other half of the dough (add a little more flour if it is too soft to grate) and spread it over the apples.

5. Bake at 375°F/190°C (Gas Mark 5) for approximately 30 minutes.

6. Serve warm with cream or custard, or cold.

CHEESE TART

Pastry:

Imperial (Metric)	American
4oz (225g) 81 per cent wholemeal flour	1 cupful 81 per cent wholewheat flour
1 teaspoonful baking powder	1 teaspoonful baking powder
Pinch sea salt	Pinch sea salt
½oz (15g) light Demerara sugar	1 tablespoonful light Demerara sugar
2oz (50g) butter *or* polyunsaturated margarine (hard)	¼ cupful butter *or* polyunsaturated margarine (hard)
1 egg, beaten	1 egg, beaten
	Pinch sea salt

1. Sift together the flour, baking powder and salt, and tip back the bran. Stir in the sugar.

2. Rub in the butter or margarine until the mixture resembles fine breadcrumbs.

3. Add the beaten egg and mix well. Add a little milk or cream to make dough firm and moist.

4. Grease an ovenproof tart dish and press the dough into it. Dust the dough with a fine layer of flour and sugar.

5. Bake blind at 375°F/190°C (Gas Mark 5) for 10-15 minutes

Filling:

Imperial (Metric)	American
2 eggs	2 eggs
1 lb (450g) cottage *or* curd cheese	1 pound cottage *or* curd cheese
⅓ pint (200ml) milk	¾ cupful milk
3oz (85g) light Demerara sugar	½ cupful light Demerara sugar
2 teaspoonsful wholemeal flour	2 teaspoonsful wholewheat flour
Pinch sea salt	Pinch sea salt

1. Beat the eggs until frothy. Set aside.

2. Beat the cottage cheese, milk and sugar together. Add the beaten eggs and beat well together.

3. Add the flour and salt and beat well again. Pour into the pastry shell.

4. Bake for 25-30 minutes at 375°F/190°C (Gas Mark 5). Delicious served warm or cold.

SABRA GLEEDA
(Ice Cream)

Imperial (Metric)	American
2 eggs	2 eggs
6oz (170g) light Demerara sugar	1 cupful light Demerara sugar
⅔ pint (340ml) milk	1½ cupsful milk
½ pint (285ml) double cream	1⅓ cupsful heavy cream
¼ pint (140ml) single cream	⅔ cupful light cream
2 teaspoonsful liqueur *or* natural vanilla flavouring	2 teaspoonsful liqueur *or* natural vanilla flavouring
Chopped nuts	Chopped nuts
Grated chocolate *or* carob bar	Grated chocolate *or* carob bar

1. Separate the egg yolks from the whites. Beat the egg whites until stiff and glossy. Set aside.

2. Combine the sugar and milk and beat well for about 10 minutes.

3. Pour both creams into the milk mixture and beat again for about 5 minutes. Add the flavouring and the yolks, beating well in.

4. Combine the beaten egg whites with the milk mixture and beat for about 5 minutes. Place in a container in the freezer.

5. After 3 or 4 hours, remove from the freezer, stir very well and mix in a few tablespoonsful of chopped nuts and grated chocolate or carob bar. Refreeze.

7. Passover

SEDER SOUP WITH MATZO KLEIS

Imperial (Metric)	American
1 large, ripe tomato, skinned	1 large, ripe tomato, skinned
2 carrots	2 carrots
1 small onion	1 small onion
2 leeks	2 leeks
2 sticks celery	2 stalks celery
1 small parsnip	1 small parsnip
1 small potato	1 small potato
8-10 cupsful water	10-12½ cupsful water
2 tablespoonsful fresh chopped parsley	2 tablespoonsful fresh chopped parsley
Sea salt and freshly ground black pepper	Sea salt and freshly ground black pepper
1 vegetable stock cube (optional)	1 vegetable stock cube (optional)

1. Wash and prepare the vegetables. Cut into small pieces.

2. Simmer the vegetables in the water for approximately 1-1½ hours.

3. Add parsley, seasonings and a vegetable soup cube if desired.

4. Serve with Matzo Kleis (page 100). Kneidlach (page 42) may also be used for Passover soups, but use only authorized Passover oil.

MATZO KLEIS

Imperial (Metric)	American
2 matzos	2 matzos
1 small onion, finely chopped	1 small onion, finely chopped
1 fl oz (30ml) vegetable oil	2 tablespoonsful vegetable oil
1 tablespoonful chopped fresh parsley	1 tablespoonful chopped fresh parsley
2 tablespoonsful ground almonds	2 tablespoonsful ground almonds
Matzo meal, fine	Matzo meal, fine
Sea salt and freshly ground black pepper	Sea salt and freshly ground black pepper
Pinch ground ginger	Pinch ground ginger
2 teaspoonsful powdered cinnamon	2 teaspoonsful powdered cinnamon
2 eggs, beaten	2 eggs, beaten

1. Leave the matzos to soak in cold water until soft. When they are quite soft, remove and squeeze out excess water. Mash the matzos well.

2. Fry the onion in vegetable oil until soft and golden.

3. Add the oil and onions to the mashed matzos.

4. Add the chopped parsley, ground almonds and seasonings, mixing well. Mix in the beaten eggs.

5. Stir in just enough matzo meal to make a firm, but not hard, consistency. Refrigerate for about one hour.

6. Make small balls, about the size of a large walnut. Dip them into fine matzo meal.

7. Boil in salted water for about 20 minutes, drain and serve with soup.

8. The uncooked balls may be placed in a vegetable casserole and baked for about 30-40 minutes. They would make a filling addition to Mushroom and Aubergine Bake (page 110) or Israeli Casserole (page 107).

SEDER ROAST

Imperial (Metric)	American
6oz (170g) mixed ground nuts	1½ cupsful mixed ground nuts
2 eggs, beaten	2 eggs, beaten
1 onion, finely chopped	1 onion, finely chopped
1-2 cloves garlic, crushed	1-2 cloves garlic, crushed
1 large carrot, grated	1 large carrot, grated
2oz (55g) matzo meal	½ cupful matzo meal
2 tablespoonsful tomato purée	2 tablespoonsful tomato paste
Sea salt and freshly ground black pepper	Sea salt and freshly ground black pepper
1 onion, sliced	1 onion, sliced
1 pint (570ml) vegetable stock	2½ cupsful vegetable stock

1. Mix together all ingredients very well, except the sliced onion and the vegetable stock.

2. Grease an ovenproof casserole well and place a layer of sliced onions on the bottom and round the sides. Place the nut mixture in the casserole.

3. Pour the vegetable stock over the mixture. Bake for about 45 minutes at 350°F/180°C (Gas Mark 4) until brown. Serve hot with vegetables or cold with salads.

Note: If this recipe is doubled, use 3 eggs instead of 4.

SEDER GRAVY

Imperial (Metric)	American
Small piece of onion	Small piece of onion
1 clove garlic	1 clove garlic
1 oz (30g) butter *or* polyunsaturated margarine	2½ tablespoonsful butter *or* polyunsaturated margarine
2 teaspoonful potato flour	2 teaspoonful potato flour
Sea salt and freshly ground black pepper	Sea salt and freshly ground black pepper
1-1½ cupsful hot vegetable stock (made with vegetable soup cube)	1¼-1¾ cupsful hot vegetable stock (made with vegetable soup cube)
1 tablespoonful red wine (optional)	1 tablespoonful red wine (optional)

1. Lightly brown the onion and garlic in melted butter or margarine. Remove the onion and garlic and take fat off heat.

2. Blend the potato flour and seasonings into the fat. Return to a low heat, browning lightly.

3. Slowly add hot stock, stirring all the time until the gravy has thickened. A tablespoonful of red wine may be added if wished. Serve with Seder Roast (page 101).

Note:

The gravy may be varied by the addition of chopped, sautéd mushrooms.

For Tomato Gravy, substitute ½ pint (285ml/1⅓ cupsful) tomato juice for vegetable stock. Add a pinch of sugar towards the end of cooking.

MERREN EN KARTOFFEL KOKLATEN

Imperial (Metric)	American
1 lb (450g) carrots	1 pound carrots
1 lb (450g) potatoes	1 pound potatoes
2 medium onions, chopped	2 medium onions, chopped
2 cloves garlic, crushed	2 cloves garlic, crushed
Vegetable oil for frying	Vegetable oil for frying
Sea salt and freshly ground black pepper	Sea salt and freshly ground black pepper
1 teaspoonful garlic salt	1 teaspoonful garlic salt
2 teaspoonsful Hungarian paprika	2 teaspoonsful Hungarian paprika
2 tablespoonsful chopped fresh parsley	2 tablespoonsful chopped fresh parsley
1 egg, beaten (optional)	1 egg, beaten (optional)
2oz (55g) fine matzo meal (or more)	½ cupful fine matzo meal (or more)

1. Peel and dice the carrots and potatoes, then boil or steam until soft.

2. Fry the chopped onions and garlic until golden-brown.

3. Mash well the carrots and potatoes and season with salt, pepper, garlic salt and paprika.

4. Add the fried onions and garlic and the oil in which they were fried. Mix well.

5. Add chopped parsley and the beaten egg, if using.

6. Mix in enough matzo meal to make a firm consistency. Add more seasoning if desired.

7. Form into rissoles, brush with oil and bake on a greased baking tray for 30-45 minutes until crisp, at 375°F/190°C (Gas Mark 5).

GEBROTTENE NISSLACH EN KARTOFFELEN

Imperial (Metric)	American
2 large onions, chopped	2 large onions, chopped
2 cloves garlic, crushed	2 cloves garlic, crushed
Vegetable oil for frying	Vegetable oil for frying
1 teaspoonful Hungarian paprika	1 teaspoonful Hungarian paprika
Sea salt and freshly ground black pepper	Sea salt and freshly ground black pepper
3-4 large ripe tomatoes, skinned and chopped	3-4 large ripe tomatoes, skinned and chopped
1 tablespoonful chopped fresh parsley	1 tablespoonful chopped fresh parsley
½ lb (225g) mixed ground nuts	2 cupsful mixed ground nuts
⅓ pint (200ml) hot vegetable stock *or* water	¾ cupful hot vegetable stock *or* water
1 lb (450g) cooked, mashed potatoes	2 cupsful cooked mashed potatoes
Polyunsaturated margarine	Polyunsaturated margarine

1. Fry the chopped onions and garlic in a little oil until golden-brown. Stir in the seasonings.

2. Add the chopped tomatoes, and cook for about 5 to 10 minutes, stirring occasionally. Add the chopped parsley and nuts and mix well.

3. Place in a greased ovenproof casserole. Pour the hot stock or water over the mixture.

4. Spoon mashed potatoes over the nut mixture. Dab with margarine.

5. Bake for about 45 minutes at 350°F/180°C (Gas Mark 4), until potatoes are browned and the mixture cooked. Delicious served with sweet and sour cabbage and beetroot.

NISSLACH KOKLATEN

Imperial (Metric)	American
1 medium onion, chopped	1 medium onion, chopped
1 clove garlic, crushed	1 clove garlic, crushed
1 stick celery, chopped	1 stalk celery, chopped
2 oz (55g) polyunsaturated margarine	¼ cupful polyunsaturated margarine
2 tablespoonsful matzo meal	2 tablespoonsful matzo meal
Sea salt and freshly ground black pepper	Sea salt and freshly ground black pepper
½ teaspoonful garlic salt	½ teaspoonful garlic salt
¼ pint (140ml) vegetable stock	⅔ cupful vegetable stock
1 egg, beaten (optional)	1 egg, beaten (optional)
½ lb (225g) ground hazelnuts or walnuts	2 cupsful ground hazelnuts or walnuts
1 tablespoonful chopped parsley	1 tablespoonful chopped parsley

1. Sauté the chopped onions, garlic and celery in the margarine.

2. Add the matzo meal and seasonings and stir well.

3. Add the stock, nuts and chopped parsley.

4. Stir well and cook for about 5 minutes. Check seasoning. Add beaten egg if using.

5. Shape into rounds. Bake on a greased baking tray at 350°F/180°C (Gas Mark 4) until browned.

CAULIFLOWER KOKLATEN

Imperial (Metric)	American
1 medium cauliflower	1 medium cauliflower
1 small onion, grated	1 small onion, grated
Vegetable oil	Vegetable oil
2oz (55g) chopped mixed nuts	½ cupful chopped mixed nuts
1 tablespoonful chopped fresh parsley	1 tablespoonful chopped fresh parsley
1½ tablespoonsful potato flour	1½ tablespoonsful potato flour
1 teaspoonful paprika	1 teaspoonful paprika
Sea salt, freshly ground black pepper and a pinch sugar	Sea salt, freshly ground black pepper and a pinch sugar
2 eggs, beaten	2 eggs, beaten
1½ teaspoonsful lemon juice	1½ teaspoonsful lemon juice

1. Wash the cauliflower well in salted water. Steam or boil until tender.

2. Fry the chopped onion in vegetable oil until golden and soft.

3. Combine the fried onion, together with the oil in which it was fried, with the chopped nuts.

4. Mash the cooked cauliflower.

5. Mix together the mashed cauliflower, nut mixture, chopped parsley, potato flour, seasonings, beaten eggs, and lemon juice.

6. Leave in refrigerator for about 20 minutes. Form into patties.

7. Place on a greased baking tray and bake at 350°F/180°C (Gas Mark 4) for about 30-45 minutes. Serve with cheese sauce or tomato gravy.

ISRAELI CASSEROLE

Imperial (Metric)	American
1 aubergine	1 eggplant
Sea salt and freshly ground black pepper	Sea salt and freshly ground black pepper
2 onions	2 onions
4 medium potatoes, parboiled (in skins)	4 medium potatoes, parboiled (in skins)
6-8 medium-sized, ripe tomatoes	6-8 medium-sized, ripe tomatoes
1 small green pepper	1 small green pepper
1 clove garlic, crushed	1 clove garlic, crushed
2 fl oz (60ml) vegetable oil	1 fl oz (60ml) vegetable oil
½ pint (285ml) hot vegetable stock	1⅓ cupsful hot vegetable stock
1 tablespoonful chopped fresh parsley	1 tablespoonful chopped fresh parsley

1. Peel the aubergine (eggplant) thinly, cut into thick slices, sprinkle with salt, and allow to stand for 30 minutes. Wash well to remove salt. Cut into smaller pieces.

2. Chop the onions, peel and dice the potatoes, skin and chop the tomatoes and de-seed and chop the green pepper.

3. Sauté the onions, green pepper and crushed garlic, for about 5 minutes.

4. Add the aubergine (eggplant) pieces and potato pieces. Sauté until soft and beginning to brown. Transfer to an ovenproof casserole with a lid.

5. Pour the vegetable stock, chopped tomatoes and parsley into the casserole. Season with sea salt and ground black pepper. Cover the casserole.

6. Bake for 30-45 minutes at 350°F/180°C (Gas Mark 4).

GOULASH WITH POTATO KNEIDLACH

Imperial (Metric)	American
2 medium onions	2 medium onions
1 small green pepper	1 small green pepper
Vegetable oil for frying	Vegetable oil for frying
2 cloves garlic, crushed	2 cloves garlic, crushed
1½ lb (675g) courgettes	1½ pounds zucchini
3-4 ripe tomatoes, medium-sized	3-4 ripe tomatoes, medium-sized
1 teaspoonful Hungarian paprika (or more)	1 teaspoonful Hungarian paprika (or more)
Sea salt and freshly ground black pepper	Sea salt and freshly ground black pepper
1 tablespoonful chopped fresh parsley	1 tablespoonful chopped fresh parsley
1-1½ cupsful hot vegetable stock	1¼-1¾ cupsful hot vegetable stock

1. Chop the onions and green pepper and fry lightly in oil together with the crushed garlic.

2. Wash and slice the courgettes (zucchini) and add to the onions and green pepper.

3. Skin and chop the tomatoes and add to the mixture. Stir in the seasonings, and the chopped parsley. Transfer to an ovenproof casserole, with lid.

4. Pour hot vegetable stock over the vegetables.

5. Put Kneidlach balls on top of the mixture.

6. Bake for about 45 minutes at 325°F/170°C (Gas Mark 3). Remove the lid and allow the Kneidlach to brown for about 20 minutes.

Kneidlach Mixture:

Imperial (Metric)	American
2 cupsful grated potatoes, uncooked	2½ cupsful grated potatoes, uncooked
1 onion, grated	1 onion, grated
2 oz (55g) matzo meal	½ cupful matzo meal
1 tablespoonful ground nuts	1 tablespoonful ground nuts
1 tablespoonful potato flour	1 tablespoonful potato flour
1 egg	1 egg
1-2 teaspoonful sea salt	1-2 teaspoonsful sea salt
Freshly ground black pepper	Freshly ground black pepper

1. Drain the liquid from the grated potatoes and add it to the vegetable stock in goulash.

2. Combine all the kneidlach ingredients, mixing well. Add more matzo meal if needed to make a firm consistency.

3. Form into balls, and place on top of goulash mixture. If the mixture is too soft, add a little more matzo meal.

If time is short, use sliced par-boiled potatoes instead of kneidlach.

COURGETTE AND LEEK CASSEROLE

Imperial (Metric)	American
4 large leeks	4 large leeks
1½ lb courgettes	1½ pounds zucchini
Vegetable oil	Vegetable oil
Sea salt and freshly ground black pepper	Sea salt and freshly ground black pepper
Garlic salt	Garlic salt

1. Cut the leeks lengthwise and wash very well under running cold water. Slice thinly. Steam or boil in a little water until soft.

2. Wash and slice the courgettes (zucchini). Sauté the courgettes (zucchini) in vegetable oil until tender.

3. In a greased casserole dish, put alternate layers of leeks and courgettes, seasoning with salt, pepper and garlic salt.

4. Cover with cheese sauce (see below). Bake for about 30 minutes at 350°F/180°C (Gas Mark 4).

Cheese Sauce:

Imperial (Metric)	American
1 oz (30g) butter *or* polyunsaturated margarine	2½ tablespoonsful butter *or* polyunsaturated margarine
1 tablespoonful potato flour	1 tablespoonful potato starch
½ pint (285ml) milk and vegetable stock, mixed	1⅓ cupsful milk and vegetable stock, mixed
Sea salt and freshly ground black pepper	Sea salt and freshly ground black pepper
½ teaspoonful nutmeg	½ teaspoonful nutmeg
2 oz (55g) grated cheese	½ cupful grated cheese

1. Melt the butter or margarine. Remove from the heat.

2. Stir in the potato flour, blending well.

3. Replace on a low heat. Add the stock and milk slowly, stirring continuously.

4. Add the seasonings and grated cheese.

MUSHROOM AND AUBERGINE BAKE

Imperial (Metric)	American
1 medium aubergine	1 medium eggplant
Sea salt and freshly ground black pepper	Sea salt and freshly ground black pepper
2 medium onions, chopped	2 medium onions, chopped
2 cloves garlic, crushed	2 cloves garlic, crushed
Vegetable oil, for frying	Vegetable oil, for frying
2 tablespoonsful tomato purée	2 tablespoonsful tomato paste
½ lb (225g) button mushrooms, chopped	3 cupsful button mushrooms, chopped
2 ripe tomatoes, skinned and chopped	2 ripe tomatoes, skinned and chopped

1. Peel and slice the aubergine (eggplant). Sprinkle cut sides with salt. Leave for 30 minutes. Wash well and drain.

2. Fry the chopped onions and garlic in oil until transparent. Stir in the tomato purée.

3. Add the aubergine (eggplant) slices and cook until soft.

4. Add the chopped mushrooms and tomatoes.

5. Season well with sea salt and black pepper. Cook for about 15 minutes.

6. Transfer to an ovenproof casserole, add a little hot water to prevent drying out. Cover and keep warm until needed, or reheat if necessary.

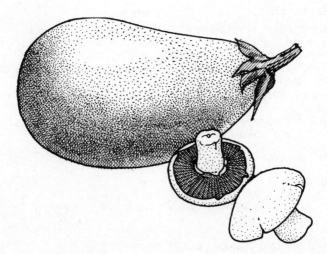

VEGETABLE BAKE

Imperial (Metric)	American
½ lb (225g) fresh spinach	8 ounces fresh spinach
2 medium onions, grated or chopped	2 medium onions, grated or chopped
1 small green pepper, de-seeded and chopped	1 small green pepper, de-seeded and chopped
1 clove garlic, crushed	1 clove garlic, crushed
Vegetable oil for frying	Vegetable oil for frying
1 stick celery, chopped	1 stalk celery, chopped
3-4 medium carrots, grated	3-4 medium carrots, grated
Sea salt and freshly ground black pepper	Sea salt and freshly ground black pepper
Pinch ginger	Pinch ginger
1 tablespoonful tomato purée	1 tablespoonful tomato purée
2 oz (55g) ground mixed nuts	½ cupful ground mixed nuts
2 eggs, beaten (optional)	2 eggs, beaten (optional)
2 oz (55g) matzo meal	¼ cupful matzo meal
3 fl oz (90ml) vegetable stock	⅓ cupful vegetable stock

1. Wash the spinach well, cook and chop finely.

2. Sauté the onions, green pepper and garlic in oil until soft.

3. Add the celery and carrots, and cook for about 10 minutes, stirring frequently.

4. Mix all the vegetables together. Add the seasonings, tomato purée, ground mixed nuts, eggs, if using, and matzo meal, mixing everything together.

5. Place in a greased ovenproof casserole, pour the hot stock over and bake for about 30 minutes until brown at 350°F/180°C (Gas Mark 4).

BROCCOLI, CHEESE AND NUT BAKE

Imperial (Metric)	American
1 lb (450g) broccoli	1 pound broccoli
2 eggs	2 eggs
½ lb (225g) cottage cheese	1 cupful cottage cheese
2 oz (55g) grated Gouda cheese	½ cupful grated Gouda cheese
3 tablespoonsful ground almonds *or* hazelnuts	3 tablespoonsful ground almonds *or* hazelnuts
2 tablespoonsful fine matzo meal	2 tablespoonsful fine matzo meal
Sea salt and freshly ground black pepper	Sea salt and freshly ground black pepper
½ teaspoonful nutmeg	½ teaspoonful nutmeg
2 tablespoonsful chopped nuts for sprinkling	2 tablespoonsful chopped nuts for sprinkling

1. Wash and divide the broccoli. Steam or cook in a little water until tender. Cut into pieces.

2. Beat the eggs well, add cottage cheese and beat together.

3. Stir in the grated Gouda, ground nuts, matzo meal and seasonings.

4. Grease an ovenproof casserole and place the cooked broccoli into it.

5. Pour the cheese and egg mixture over the broccoli. Bake for about 20 minutes at 350°F/180°C (Gas Mark 4). Remove from oven. Sprinkle with chopped nuts. Bake for a further 10-15 minutes.

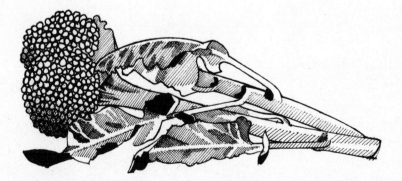

SAVOURY MATZO BAKE

Imperial (Metric)	American
1 medium onion, chopped	1 medium onion, chopped
1 clove garlic, crushed	1 clove garlic, crushed
1 small green pepper, de-seeded and chopped	1 small green pepper, de-seeded and chopped
Vegetable oil for frying	Vegetable oil for frying
4-5 ripe tomatoes, skinned and chopped	4-5 ripe tomatoes, skinned and chopped
Sea salt and freshly ground black pepper	Sea salt and freshly ground black pepper
Garlic salt	Garlic salt
*1 teaspoon sugar	*1 teaspoon sugar
2 tablespoonsful chopped fresh parsley	2 tablespoonsful chopped fresh parsley
5-6 matzos	5-6 matzos
2oz (55g) grated cheese	½ cupful grated cheese
Sliced mushrooms for garnishing	Sliced mushrooms for garnishing
2 eggs	2 eggs
⅓ pint (200ml) hot vegetable stock	¾ cupful hot vegetable stock

1. Fry the onion, garlic and green pepper in oil until soft and golden.

2. Add the chopped tomatoes and seasonings, and cook for a further 10 minutes. Add chopped parsley.

3. Dip the matzos in water to moisten, but not soften.

4. Place one matzo in the bottom of a greased ovenproof casserole. Spoon some of the onion and tomato mixture over it. Sprinkle grated cheese over the mixture.

5. Repeat until all the matzos, sauce and cheese have been used. Top with sliced mushrooms.

6. Beat the eggs well and mix with hot stock. Pour over the layered matzos.

7. Bake at 350°F/180°C (Gas Mark 4) for about 30-40 minutes.

*As raw cane sugar is not generally available for Passover use, it is not specified in any Passover recipes.

GEBAKENE KARTOFFEL MIT KAESE

Imperial (Metric)	American
2 lb (900g) potatoes	2 pounds potatoes
½ lb (225g) cottage cheese	1 cupful cottage cheese
2 spring onions, finely chopped	2 scallions, finely chopped
2 tablespoonsful chopped fresh parsley	2 tablespoonsful chopped fresh parsley
½ pint (285ml) milk	1⅓ cupful milk
Sea salt and freshly ground black pepper	Sea salt and freshly ground black pepper
½ teaspoonful nutmeg	½ teaspoonful nutmeg
3 tablespoonsful grated Gouda cheese	3 tablespoonsful grated Gouda cheese

1. Boil the potatoes in their jackets until cooked. Peel, and cut into small pieces.

2. Mix together the rest of the ingredients, except the grated cheese.

3. Grease an ovenproof casserole and place alternate layers of potatoes and cheese mixture into it. Add grated cheese to the final layer.

4. Bake for about 20-30 minutes at 350°F/180°C (Gas Mark 4) until golden-brown. This dish is nice served with tomatoes stuffed with broccoli and chopped nuts, (page 117).

GEMÜSE

Imperial (Metric)	American
4 oz (115g) button mushrooms	2 cupful button mushrooms
1 medium to large aubergine	1 medium to large eggplant
4 oz (115g) matzo meal	1 cupful matzo meal
1 teaspoonful garlic powder	1 teaspoonful garlic powder
1 teaspoonful paprika	1 teaspoonful paprika
Sea salt and freshly ground black pepper	Sea salt and freshly ground black pepper
1 egg	1 egg
Vegetable oil	Vegetable oil

1. Wash the mushrooms well, but do not cut them up.

2. Peel the aubergine (eggplant) thinly, slice and sprinkle cut sides with salt.

3. Leave for about 30 minutes, wash salt off, rinse well, drain and pat dry with kitchen paper.

4. Combine the matzo meal with seasonings. Beat the egg very well.

5. Dip the vegetable slices and mushrooms alternately in matzo meal, beaten egg, and again in matzo meal.

6. Fry in the vegetable oil until golden-brown.

7. Place on kitchen paper until excess oil has drained away.

MERREN TZIMMES

Imperial (Metric)	American
2 medium onions, grated or finely chopped	2 medium onions, grated or finely chopped
2 cloves garlic, crushed	2 cloves garlic, crushed
2 tablespoonsful vegetable oil	2 tablespoonsful vegetable oil
1 lb (450g) carrots, grated	1 pound carrots, grated
3 tablespoonsful ground almonds	3 tablespoonsful ground almonds
1 teaspoonful lemon juice	1 teaspoonful lemon juice
1 egg, beaten	1 egg, beaten
Sea salt and freshly ground black pepper	Sea salt and freshly ground black pepper
¼ teaspoonful ground nutmeg	¼ teaspoonful ground nutmeg
2oz (55g) matzo meal	½ cupful matzo meal

1. Fry the grated onion and garlic in the oil until golden and transparent.

2. Add the grated carrots, stirring continuously, and cook for another 5 minutes. Remove from the heat.

3. Combine with the ground almonds, lemon juice, egg and seasonings, mixing well.

4. Add enough matzo meal to make a firm consistency.

5. Put in a greased ovenproof casserole and bake for about 30 minutes at 375°F/190°C (Gas Mark 5).

TZIBBALE KUGEL

Imperial (Metric)	American
4 medium onions, finely chopped or grated	4 medium onions, finely chopped or grated
2 fl oz (60ml) vegetable oil	¼ cupful vegetable oil
4 eggs, separated	4 eggs, separated
2oz (55g) matzo meal	½ cupful matzo meal
1 teaspoonful sea salt	1 teaspoonful sea salt
Freshly ground black pepper	Freshly ground black pepper
¼ teaspoonful ground ginger	¼ teaspoonful ground ginger

1. Sauté onions in oil until golden and transparent.

2. Beat the egg yolks until thick and creamy.

3. Mix in sautéd onions, oil, matzo meal and seasonings, combining everything well together.

4. Beat the egg whites until stiff and fold into onion mixture.

5. Bake in well-greased ovenproof dish for about 30-40 minutes at 350°F/180°C (Gas Mark 4).

BURRIKLACH MIT MERRALACH

Imperial (Metric)	American
3 medium beetroots, uncooked	3 medium beets, uncooked
3 carrots	3 carrots
2 eating apples	2 eating apples
2 tablespoonsful olive oil	2 tablespoonsful olive oil
1 tablespoonful lemon juice	1 tablespoonful lemon juice
Sea salt and freshly ground black pepper	Sea salt and freshly ground black pepper
2 tablespoonsful chopped fresh parsley	2 tablespoonsful chopped fresh parsley

1. Peel and grate the beetroots (beets), carrots and apples.

2. Mix the olive oil, lemon juice and seasonings together, and pour over the salad. Add more oil and lemon juice if liked.

3. Sprinkle with chopped parsley.

4. Delicious with Koklaten (pages 103-106) and Nut Roasts.

STUFFED TOMATOES

Imperial (Metric)	American
4-6 firm tomatoes	4-6 firm tomatoes
4oz (115g) broccoli	4 ounces broccoli
Olive oil, mixed with lemon juice, to taste	Olive oil, mixed with lemon juice, to taste
1 tablespoonful chopped parsley	1 tablespoonful chopped parsley
Sea salt and freshly ground black pepper	Sea salt and freshly ground black pepper
Pinch sugar	Pinch sugar
2 tablespoonsful chopped nuts	2 tablespoonsful chopped nuts

1. Cut the tops off the tomatoes and scoop out the pulp. Allow the tomatoes to drain.

2. Wash and steam or boil the broccoli until tender. Cut into small pieces. Toss with the olive oil, lemon juice, parsley and seasonings. Stir in about 2 tablespoonsful of the tomato pulp. (Reserve the remaining tomato pulp for use in soups and casseroles.)

3. Pile the mixture into the tomato shells. Sprinkle with chopped nuts just before serving.

4. Serve cold or topped with cheese sauce (page 109) or grated cheese and baked for about 25-30 minutes in a moderate oven.

GESHMIRTE MATZO

Imperial (Metric)	American
Matzo crackers *or* large matzos	Matzo crackers *or* large matzos
2 fl oz (60ml) cream *or* milk	¼ cupful cream *or* milk
½ lb (225g) cottage cheese	1 cupful cottage cheese
1½ teaspoonsful potato flour	1½ teaspoonsful potato starch
1 egg, beaten	1 egg, beaten
1 oz (30g) sugar	2 tablespoonsful sugar
Pinch sea salt	Pinch sea salt
Powdered cinnamon	Powdered cinnamon
Extra sugar and cinnamon, to taste	Extra sugar and cinnamon, to taste

1. Dip the matzos in the cream or milk and remove quickly, as they need to be moistened but not softened.

2. Mix the rest of the ingredients together very well including any remaining cream or milk. Spread the mixture over the matzos.

3. Sprinkle with extra cinnamon and a little more sugar.

4. Bake at 350°F/180°C (Gas Mark 4) until lightly set. Serve warm.

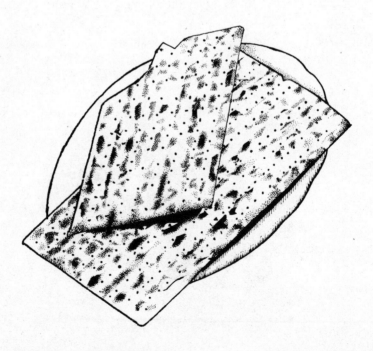

MATZO LATKES

Imperial (Metric)	American
4oz (115g) matzo meal	½ cupful matzo meal
1½ tablespoonsful ground almonds *or* hazelnuts	1½ tablespoonsful ground almonds *or* hazelnuts
1 tablespoonful sugar	1 tablespoonful sugar
½ teaspoonful powdered cinnamon	½ teaspoonful powdered cinnamon
Sea salt	Sea salt
2 eggs, separated	2 eggs, separated
⅓ pint (200ml) cold water	¾ cupful cold water
Vegetable oil for frying	Vegetable oil for frying

1. Mix together the matzo meal, ground nuts, sugar and seasonings. Make a well in the centre.

2. Beat the egg yolks, add water and beat again.

3. Add the egg and water mixture to the matzo meal mixture, mixing well. Leave for about 15 minutes.

4. Beat the egg whites, but not too stiffly. Mix them into the matzo meal mixture.

5. Heat the oil in a frying pan (skillet) and fry spoonsful of the mixture, browning on both sides. Serve hot with extra powdered cinnamon and a little sugar.

APPLE LATKES

Imperial (Metric)	American
3 medium eating apples	3 medium eating apples
2oz (55g) matzo meal	½ cupful matzo meal
1½ tablespoonsful sugar	1½ tablespoonsful sugar
2 eggs, beaten	2 eggs, beaten
Pinch ground cinnamon	Pinch ground cinnamon
Sea salt	Sea salt
Vegetable oil for frying	Vegetable oil for frying

1. Peel the apples and grate them.

2. Combine the grated apples with the rest of the ingredients except the oil, mixing everything well together. Add 1-2 tablespoonsful cold water, stirring in.

3. Refrigerate for about 20 minutes.

4.. Drop in spoonsful into a lightly oiled frying pan. Brown on both sides.

5. Drain on kitchen or brown paper.

6. Serve hot sprinkled with powdered cinnamon and sugar.

LAYERED MATZO PUDDING

Imperial (Metric)	American
4-5 eating apples	4-5 eating apples
4 matzos	4 matzos
3oz (85g) raisins, washed in hot water	½ cupful raisins, washed in hot water
2oz (55g) butter or polyunsaturated margarine	¼ cupful butter or polyunsaturated margarine
2 eggs	2 eggs
1oz (30g) sugar	2 tablespoonsful sugar
¾ pint (425ml) water or milk	2 cupsful water or milk
Pinch sea salt	Pinch sea salt
1 teaspoonful ground cinnamon	1 teaspoonful ground cinnamon
3 tablespoonsful chopped nuts	3 tablespoonsful chopped nuts

1. Grate the apples, or slice very thinly.

2. Dip the matzos in water to moisten, but not soften. Place one matzo in bottom of greased pie dish.

3. Place a layer of grated apples on top of the matzo and sprinkle with raisins. Dot with pieces of butter or margarine.

4. Repeat until the matzos, apples and butter or margarine have been used.

5. Beat the eggs and sugar until frothy. Add water or milk, salt and cinnamon. Pour over the layers in the pie dish.

6. Sprinkle with chopped nuts. Dab with more butter or margarine.

7. Bake for about 20-30 minutes at 350°F/180°C (Gas Mark 4).

MATZO APPLE MERINGUE

Imperial (Metric)	American
5-6 sweet eating apples	5-6 sweet eating apples
3 eggs	3 eggs
1 oz (30g) sugar	2 tablespoonsful sugar
4 tablespoonsful orange juice	4 tablespoonsful orange juice
4 oz (225g) fine matzo meal	1 cupful fine matzo meal
1 oz (30g) sugar for meringue (or more)	2 tablespoonful sugar for meringue (or more)
Ground almonds	Ground almonds

1. Grate the apples.

2. Separate the egg yolks from the whites.

3. Beat the egg yolks and sugar together until light. Add orange juice.

4. Stir in the matzo meal and the grated apples.

5. Place in a greased pie dish and bake for about 30-40 minutes at 350°F/180°C (Gas Mark 4).

6. Beat the egg whites with a pinch of salt until stiff, adding sugar gradually.

7. Spread this over the cooked apple cake mixture and sprinkle with ground almonds.

8. Reduce the oven temperature to 325°F/170°C (Gas Mark 3). Bake until the meringue is golden-brown.

PESACH APPLE AND NUT PUDDING

Imperial (Metric)	American
4 eggs	4 eggs
Sea salt	Sea salt
4oz (115g) sugar	⅔ cupful sugar
3-4 eating apples, grated	3-4 eating apples, grated
Grated lemon rind	Grated lemon rind
1oz (30g) matzo meal	¼ cupful matzo meal
1oz (30g) ground almonds	¼ cupful ground almonds
3-4 tablespoonsful chopped almonds	3-4 tablespoonsful chopped almonds

1. Separate the egg yolks and whites. Beat the whites with a pinch of salt until stiff. Set aside.

2. Beat the yolks and sugar together until light and creamy. Add grated apples, lemon rind, matzo meal and ground almonds. Fold in the egg whites.

3. Place in a greased pie dish. Sprinkle with chopped almonds. Bake for about 40 minutes at 350°F/180°C (Gas Mark 4).

PLAVAH
(Passover Cake)

Imperial (Metric)	American
4 eggs	4 eggs
6oz (170g) powdered sugar	1 cupful powdered sugar
2 teaspoonsful lemon juice	2 teaspoonsful lemon juice
3oz (85g) fine matzo meal	¾ cupful fine matzo meal
Pinch sea salt	Pinch sea salt

1. Separate the egg yolks and whites. Beat the yolks and sugar until pale and creamy.

2. Add the lemon juice, matzo meal, and pinch salt.

3. Beat whites until stiff. Fold into cake mixture.

4. Bake in a paper-lined greased tin for about 40-45 minutes at 350°F/180°C (Gas Mark 4) until golden and cooked. Test by inserting a knife or toothpick. If it comes out dry, the cake is done.

5. Dust with castor sugar.

Variation:
Bake in two sandwich tins for about 25-30 minutes. Sandwich together with whipped cream and crushed strawberries.

PESACH CHOCOLATE NUT SQUARES

Imperial (Metric)	American
2 eggs	2 eggs
5oz (140g) sugar	¾ cupful sugar
1 tablespoonful Sabra liqueur (optional)	1 tablespoonful Sabra liqueur (optional)
2oz (55g) dark chocolate	2 ounces dark chocolate
4oz (115g) butter *or* polyunsaturated margarine	½ cupful butter *or* polyunsaturated margarine
2oz (55g) fine matzo cake meal	½ cupful fine matzo meal
3oz (85g) chopped nuts	⅔ cupful chopped nuts
Pinch sea salt	Pinch sea salt

1. Beat the eggs and sugar together until light and creamy. Add the liqueur if using and beat again.

2. Melt the chocolate in a saucepan over slowly boiling water.

3. Add butter or margarine, melt and mix well. Allow to cool (place saucepan into basin of cold water for a few minutes).

4. Combine the cooled chocolate mixture with the egg mixture.

5. Add the matzo meal a little at a time, stirring well. Add salt and nuts.

6. Bake in a well greased tin for about 20-30 minutes at 325°F/170°C (Gas Mark 3). Cut into squares while warm.

Note: The recipe may be varied by adding a little grated orange peel.

INGBERLACH
(Sweets/Candies)

Imperial (Metric)	American
1½lb (675g) carrots	1½ pounds carrots
1lb (450g) sugar	1 pound sugar
⅓ pint (200ml) orange juice	¾ cupful orange juice
½ teaspoonful ground cinnamon	½ teaspoonful ground cinnamon
1½ teaspoonsful ground ginger	1½ teaspoonsful ground ginger
4oz (115g) ground or chopped nuts	1 cupful ground or chopped nuts

1. Scrape the carrots, dice and steam or boil in a little water until tender. Mash very finely and squeeze out excess water.

2. On a very low heat, cook the mashed carrots, orange juice, sugar, cinnamon and ginger. Stir often to prevent sticking. After about 20 minutes, add the nuts.

3. Cook for about 10 more minutes, stirring often. Remove from heat. The mixture should be fairly thick.

4. Dampen a pastry board. Spread the mixture to a thickness of about ½ inch (1cm). When cold, cut into squares, sprinkle with sugar and serve as sweets.

ABOUT THE INTERNATIONAL JEWISH VEGETARIAN SOCIETY

The International Jewish Vegetarian Society, which is represented in over a dozen countries, welcomes mew members from all parts of the world. The quarterly magazine, sent free to members, features articles on nutrition, health, travel, gardening, recipes, ethical and religious aspects of vegetarianism, with news from and about its many readers, as well as giving information about international developments and conferences.

Further information regarding membership of the Society, and enquiries about matters related to this book, can be directed to the International Jewish Vegerarian Society's Headquarters, Bet Teva, 853/855 Finchley Road, London NW11 8LX (S.A.E., please).

INDEX